Theology for the 1980s

Theology
for the 1980s

By
JOHN CARMODY

THE WESTMINSTER PRESS

Philadelphia

BOOK DESIGN BY DOROTHY ALDEN SMITH

First edition

Published by The Westminster Press®
Philadelphia, Pennsylvania

PRINTED IN THE UNITED STATES OF AMERICA
9 8 7 6 5 4 3 2 1

Library of Congress Cataloging in Publication Data

Carmody, John, 1939–
    Theology for the 1980s.

    Bibliography: p.
    Includes index.
    1. Theology—20th century. I. Title.
BT28.C35   230'.09'047   80–19349
ISBN 0–664–24345–2

For my sister
Joann Carmody Corlett

Contents

Preface

Numerous friends and fellow workers in the field of religion helped in this project, and I want to acknowledge them here. The Institute for Ecumenical and Cultural Research, Collegeville, Minnesota, provided an optimal place to work during the summer of 1978. I should like to thank the president of the Institute, Kilian McDonnell, and its staff, Robert S. Bilheimer, Dolores Schuh, and Wilfred Theisen, for kindnesses beyond the terms of the contract. I should like to thank as well my co-fellows, Patrick Henry, Herbert Huffmon, and Donald Klinefelter, for support and helpful comments. David Hollenbach, Mary E. Hunt, and Jon M. Nilson sent help through the mails. My colleagues in the religion department at Wichita State University, Robert Goldenberg, Jerry Irish, Michael Kalton, Howard Mickel, Judith Plaskow, David Suter, and Paul Wiebe, made miscellaneous important contributions. Robert McAfee Brown bridged my way to The Westminster Press, and its staff made me feel at home there. Denise Lardner Carmody was the unrecording angel behind this as all my books. Such a list of supporters shows quite concretely that no writer is an island. To all of them my thanks.

J.C.

CHAPTER 1

Introduction

A BRIEF RETROSPECTIVE

Since the turn of the century, Christian theology has undergone the same rapid evolution that has marked the great historical entities of our culture. Protestant theology especially has experienced a very dramatic series of shifts. Early in the century, "liberal" theologians emphasized humanistic aspects of faith, at least in part as a continuation of nineteenth-century secularization, but also as a theological participation in the belief in "progress" that prevailed before World War I. Liberal theologians, in their different ways, concentrated on the ethical program they found in Jesus' preaching, "the brotherhood of man and the fatherhood of God" being one slogan summarizing their view. Specifically on the American scene, the social gospel, of which Walter Rauschenbusch was a principal proponent, launched liberalism as an attack on poverty, ignorance, and injustice, looking upon the church as an agent for America's sociocultural improvement.

The experience of two world wars and a major depression cost Protestant theologians much of their previous optimism. Stunned by human incorrigibility, they turned to their roots in the Bible and the Reformation. In this sense, "neo-orthodoxy" amounted to retrieving the primacy of God's Word. Karl Barth laid out the dogmatic implications of this primacy in volume after volume of rich exegesis. The movement toward church reunion came to center an ecumenical faith in the proposition that Jesus Christ is Lord. In the United States, the brothers Reinhold and H. Richard Niebuhr pioneered a new realism about social disorder and the trials of faith in industrial times.

By the mid-1970s, Protestant theology had developed well beyond neo-orthodoxy. Those who had sat at the feet of Barth, the Niebuhrs, Bultmann, and Tillich both continued their established programs and achieved a critical perspective on them. In biblical scholarship, Bultmann's exegesis gave way to a self-conscious interest in hermeneutics, the study of interpretation—that is, how we determine what a scriptural text or cultural artifact means. As both historians and philosophers took a hermeneutical "turn," Protestant theology found that neither "history" nor "meaning of life" were simple terms. Similarly, God's "Word" assumed a greater richness of meaning as well as a greater ambiguity, because advances in hermeneutics showed it to be more deeply immersed in human experience than previous generations had thought. This ambiguity affected the "death of God" theology of the 1960s, the political positions and counterpositions of the late '60s and early '70s, and the evangelical surge that is with us yet. Whether by immersing theologians in the genuine complexity of interpretation, or by releasing them to the equally genuine need that people have to see their way clear to act, hermeneutics set the Protestant tone at the end of the '70s. In church and university theology alike, the faith that seeks understanding kept grappling with the meaning of faith's language, its story, and its divinity.

Roman Catholic theology began the twentieth century with the dogmatic, neo-scholastic mentality given it by Vatican I and Pope Leo XIII's renovation of Thomism. Through the first half of the century, biblical and liturgical studies gained momentum, and a revival of interest in patristics sponsored the "nouvelle theologie" of French Catholicism after World War II. Neo-Thomist philosophy developed in various ways. The moderate realism of Étienne Gilson read the history of modern thought as an oscillation between empiricism and idealism. More subjectively oriented thinkers like Joseph Maréchal labored to reconcile Thomism with Kantian and Hegelian insights.

These movements interacted vigorously at the Second Vatican Council. The impact of the scriptural and liturgical renaissances was obvious at the Council, but the new openness to modernity was the work of the theologians Karl Rahner, Hans Küng, Yves Congar, Edward Schillebeeckx, and John Courtney Murray. They provided the bridge that allowed a very tradition-conscious church to meet the contemporary world more sympathetically. In degrees on the church, religious liberty, the church in the modern world, and revelation, the Council showed the church willing to see God's work outside its own institutional boundaries. *Aggiornamento,* or renewal, was indeed Pope John XXIII's watchword.

In the United States, Catholic theology only started to come of age immediately prior to Vatican II. Until that time, it was largely directed to the needs of an immigrant population rather than to those of an educated middle class. Further, before Vatican II, Roman authorities kept a close eye on Catholic theologians, and Pius XII's encyclical *Humani Generis* (1950) regarded evolution and existentialism quite skeptically. Partly in consequence, the American clergy did not have a strong tradition of adventurous scholarship. Still, many of them came to feel their pluralistic situation more valuable than their European superiors did. This feeling flowered in Vatican II's decree on religious liberty, where "the American experience" helped the church come to terms with this pluralism.

Since Vatican II, Catholic theology has developed a great variety of concerns. Systematicians such as Karl Rahner and Bernard Lonergan have continued to work "to augment and perfect the old by the new." In pursuit of this goal Rahner has struggled with a staggering variety of doctrinal questions from what might be called an existential Thomist's point of view. Lonergan has labored at the more foundational task of reconceiving theology as a collaboration among functional specialties.

In other fields, Catholic scholarship has become thoroughly ecumenical. Scripture, historical theology, and liturgical studies are in constant dialogue with Protestant and other scholarship. From both European and Latin-American sources, Catholic theology has also grown more political. Its liberation thought derives in good part from Marxism, and leftist Catholic theologians probably feel they have more in common with leftist Protestants than with Catholics of the right.

Eastern Orthodoxy is rarely treated in depth in American discussions of contemporary Christianity. In part, this is because in this century Orthodoxy has had only a minor impact on the European and American theological scenes. In part also it is because Orthodoxy's political fortunes in native locales such as Greece, Russia, and Eastern Europe have sapped the energies that creating a vigorous theology demands. Nonetheless, a solid corps of Orthodox thinkers have tried to clarify what modernity means for the Eastern Church. Some of them, Solovyev, Berdyaev, and Bulgakov, are now fairly familiar in the West. As

Americans know from reading Tolstoy and Dostoevsky, prerevolutionary Russia had also developed a profound spirituality, which has helped many Russians, both native and émigré, to cope with their political and economic difficulties. The same is true of the Greeks, for whom the asceticism of Mt. Athos continues to keep mystical theology alive.

Orthodox liturgy, both Russian and Greek, has comforted the faithful with its beauty and attracted many non-Orthodox. In the figure of the *starets,* or spiritual father, and in hesychasm, or inner silence, Orthodoxy continues in the tradition of the Jesus prayer.[1] As information about religious activities has become more available, we have realized the continuing importance of Christianity for contemporary Russians. The preaching of Fr. Dmitrii Dudko, prominent for his success before being silenced, manifests this in a simple, quite realistic way. In the United States, Orthodox theology cannot compete with that of Protestants and Roman Catholics, but Orthodox theologians such as John Meyendorff and Alexander Schmemann have become respected, as has the publishing program of their seminary, St. Vladimir's in Crestwood, New York.

In the last fifteen years or so Christian theology has become increasingly ecumenical. In 1966 William Hordern could say of ecumenical dialogue that it was so new as not yet to have made a significant impact upon Protestant theology as a whole.[2] But in 1978 Robert McAfee Brown, who pioneered that dialogue in his book with Gustave Weigel, wrote a liberation theology largely on Roman Catholic sources.[3] Correspondingly, David Tracy, whose *Blessed Rage for Order* established him as perhaps the leader among younger American Catholic theologians, quoted Protestant authors as freely as Catholic.[4] Clearly, since Hordern's time theology has taken a new direction. Today while a given theologian's particular religious tradition may continue to shape his or her work, it is probably less influential than the problems such work treats.

THEOLOGICAL METHOD: RECENT DISCUSSION

When Pascal had God say, "You would not seek me had you not already found me," he might well have had in mind the preoccupation with theological method so prevalent in the 1970s and, most likely, in the 1980s as well.

A work that thoroughly illustrates this hermeneutical preoccupation is Julian N. Hartt's *Theological Method and Imagination.* In it, Hartt deals with topics that now bedevil all speculative theologians: the relationship of faith to reason, scriptural authority, revelation, the uses of history, the theology of story, and more. As with the David Tracy volume mentioned above, the context of Hartt's argument is the contemporary secular horizon, wherein so many of the beliefs, symbols, and creedal statements of traditional Christian faith seem to miscarry. In language sometimes quite eloquent, Hartt demonstrates first that recent studies of language, especially those of Wittgenstein, demand a high degree of sophistication from any theologian who is going to make strong claims about what scriptural or traditional texts mean. Second, that there is an objectivity, an intending of something real, apart from which faith, theology, and Scripture lose their whole reason to be. In other words, they cannot be simply "symbolic" in the sense of nonobjective. In his own words:

> There is another and far loftier objective of theology. That is to discover and propagate the truth about ultimate reality. This must be the first and highest aim, the divine responsibility of theological thinking.

An alternate version specifies what this means for Christian theology:

> I reiterate that the primary goal of that theology called Christian is to amplify the power to see God in all things and thus to participate in the superabundance of his being.[5]

The contemporary state of consciousness, so aware that a great variety of factors affect our sense of God, warrants both Hartt's complicated analyses of interpretation and his need to argue that theology intends realities not entirely of the mind's own making. These are the ecumenical assets of his work.

Another set of proposals for restructuring theology is that of Gordon Kaufman. *An Essay on Theological Method* is a lucid statement in three parts: the proper business of theology, theology as construction, and the three "moments" of theological construction. Beginning with the first, the proper business of theology is to explicate the meaning of the word "God":

> Theology as an activity and a discipline appears when critical attention is devoted to this word and the complex of meanings associated with it. The central business of theology is reflection on the peculiar weightiness and meaning involved in the term "God" with a view to determining as explicitly, precisely, and coherently as possible just what that meaning is and what its implications are.

For Kaufman, reflection on "God" ought to issue in a work of artistic imagination:

> The theologian's task is to construct a conception or picture of the world—the whole that contains all that is and all that can be conceived—as pervaded by and purveying a particular kind of [humane] meaning and significance because of its grounding in an ultimately

humane reality. In this respect the theologian is essentially an artist; and the activity of imaginative unifying
and ordering in which he or she is engaged is to some
extent controlled by aesthetic considerations of harmony and balance, consistency and contrast. However, unlike much art, theology does not confine itself
to this or that segment or fragment of experience,
attempting to set it forth clearly and distinctly, but
rather addresses itself to the *whole* within which all
experience falls.

Finally, theological construction involves three "moments":

> The first step is the imaginative move beyond the
> items and objects of experience itself to construct a
> notion of the context within which all experience falls,
> a concept of the world; the second step is the further
> constructive leap which limits and relativizes this con-
> cept of the world through generation of the concept
> of God; finally, there is the third imaginative move
> which returns again to experience and the world,
> thoroughly reconceiving them now in the light of this
> concept of God, i.e., grasping them theologically.[6]

Concerning critical foundations, Kaufman explicitly opposes the notions of a supervening revelation providing
the theologian his or her point of vantage. Rather, all our
talk about "God" is of sociocultural origins, at least in the
sense that (1) our first use of this word is an uncritical one
and (2) nonbelievers use it equally intelligibly. Thus, "God
talk" must begin from "below," that is, it must stay close
to human experience. Kaufman buttresses these assertions
with a theory of human consciousness, owing much to
Kant, which does not try to treat "world" or "God" as
though they were objects of direct perception. His "three-
fold movement" is reminiscent of the "true method of
discovery" that Whitehead likened to an airplane: taxiing

on the ground of experience, rising to imaginative generalization, and returning to the ground to test its speculation for its payoff in insight and utility.[7]

Kaufman does not focus his scheme for Christian, Jewish, or Muslim theologians. He is, rather, trying to "isolate
and uncover certain features of the basic logical structure
of all [monotheistic] talk about God, whether Jewish or
Catholic or Methodist."[8] Nor does he pay much attention
either to the subtopics of a given theology, including perhaps human sociability in terms of church, synagogue, or
Muslim community, or to the concrete practice of a life of
faith in the reality whose meaning theology labors to illu-
minate. He grants that the subtopics are legitimate, and
that the illumination of "God" has existential causes and
repercussions, but elucidating theology's core task is the
principal aim of his essay.

In response to Kaufman, one might well ask whether (1)
"God" and "world" are the only primal concepts with
which theology must deal, (2) Christian theology must not
focus on Jesus, who presumably recasts its notions of all
primary realities, since they become most luminous
through faith in him, (3) constructive theology must not
deal with the entire theological field, since (following Lonergan) research, interpretation, history, dialectics, doctrines, and communications are equally functional
specialities, and (4) below the "God" of human construction lies the God of "revelation," the divine reality which
historically has moved both mystics and philosophers.

Kaufman's desire to stay close to human experience is a
congenial one—the experience that carries the symbols of
faith, and the working experience of the theological con-
structivist. The same desire permeates such other recent
treatments of theological method as David Tracy's *Blessed
Rage for Order* and Bernard Lonergan's *Method in Theol-*

ogy. Tracy begins his work with two principal assumptions: first, that the present pluralism of theology can be enriching, and second, that "each theologian must attempt to articulate and defend an explicit method of inquiry, and use that method to interpret the symbols and texts of our common life and of Christianity."[9] The first assumption commits Tracy to drawing on several theological traditions, to the "ecumenism" I discussed above, and the second to a "revisionist" effort to make theology analogous to other disciplines that have come of critical age, and built foundations on human reason.

Tracy's revisionism includes five theses. First, the two principal sources for Christian theology are the Christian texts and common human experience and language. Second, after theology has investigated these two sources, it must "correlate" its findings. Such correlation owes a debt to Paul Tillich, for Tracy shares Tillich's desire to set Christian symbols and present culture in dialogue. Third, investigating common human experience and language implies developing a phenomenology of the religious dimension that science, everyday experience, and everyday language carry. Fourth, investigating Christian texts (or tradition) implies history and hermeneutics. Fifth, theology should determine the truth status of its results through a transcendental or metaphysical reflection, a validation of their standing in reality.

Behind these five theses lies an uncommon labor to grasp how theology has functioned in the past, especially the most recent past. Tracy's revisionism thus constitutes an effort to advance beyond such predecessors as the "orthodoxy" of Vatican I Catholic theology, the liberal theology of Schleiermacher, the neo-orthodoxy of Barth, Tillich, and Rahner, and the radical theology of van Buren, Hamilton, and Altizer. The current pluralism of our culture requires such an advance, for unless we revise theology's horizon we cannot make sense of the many apparently conflicting insights in contemporary faith. Neither will we match the critical standards of scholarship in other fields.

The strength of Tracy's work is its familiarity with recent theological history, both Protestant and Catholic, and its drive toward critical foundations. By focusing on the correlation of real Christian faith and common human experience, Tracy creates a "humanistic" theology: a scholarly, rational reflection that aims at disclosing how and why the Christian past can be decisively meaningful to the common present. While those who find the Christian religion more mysterious and common human experience less rational may think Tracy overdoes the critical component, Tracy's interest in both the canonical symbols of the Christian past and the concrete consciousness of contemporary life is both healthy and necessary. Without making contemporary consciousness superior to Christian faith, or making Christian faith itself the only way to sanity, we can still say that their correlation is absolutely essential.

Tracy gets much of his drive toward a critical, methodologically sophisticated theology from Bernard Lonergan. Indeed, his first book traced Lonergan's theological "achievement," in terms of his development from the medieval horizon of Aquinas to that of modern historical studies. Although *Blessed Rage for Order* departs from Lonergan by embracing a process notion of God, still there are tacit debts to Lonergan on almost every page, and Tracy makes no effort to disguise them.

Two years after Tracy's book on his work appeared, Lonergan finally published *Method in Theology,* the product of a long and careful process of constant redesign. The text is divided into two parts, background and foreground. The background summarizes and enlarges upon his work on cognitional theory and meaning in *Insight* some fifteen years earlier. In essence, it describes how our awareness, our consciousness, structures itself and pursues meaning. Such self-structuring becomes directive for theology when Lonergan gets to the foreground, as we shall see momentarily. Right now it is enough to note that *(a)* consciousness consists of four interlocking stages or levels: experience, understanding, judgment, and decision, and *(b)* it finds fulfillment in religion, which Lonergan describes as the authenticity, the self-transcendence, that comes from being in love with God, being in love unrestrictedly.[10]

Religion is the raw material of theology, because "theology mediates between a cultural matrix and the role of a religion in that matrix."[11] Thus, Lonergan's theology is one of correlation between the Christian specification of being in love with God and the given culture in which that love would express itself, the given culture which that love would clarify and save. To make such a correlation critically and comprehensively, theology in its foreground or workday garb ought to coordinate eight "functional specialties." That is, it ought to respond to the complexities and differentiations of modern culture by dividing its work into eight subconcentrations.

In a "mediat*ing*" or listening phase, theology should (1) research its primary sources, (2) interpret them, (3) compose the history, the flowing actuality, that the sources reveal, and (4) determine dialectically the horizon and critical foundation in virtue of which such actuality is the way, the truth, and the life. In a "mediat*ed*" or speaking phase, theology should (5) explicate the choice or self-commission that gives its foundations. Then, it can (6) expose such a choice's (faith's) doctrines, (7) attempt to systematize them (order them hypothetically, by creative imagination), and (8) communicate their intelligible riches to a given culture or time.[12]

On the whole, *Method in Theology* addresses professional theologians concerned about the infrastructure of their discipline. The lay person or pastor interested in bread-and-butter issues can only have faith that functional specialization and collaboration could bear pastoral fruit. The principal bequests of *Method in Theology* to the 1980s are its resolute correlation of religion and culture, its clarification of theology's foundations in conversion and authenticity, and its closeness to faith's intentionality, that is, to faith's passion to give itself in unrestricted love.

THEOLOGICAL METHOD AND THE TASK OF THIS BOOK

Perhaps the method most appropriate for an investigation such as this is that proposed by Eric Voegelin. In *Order and History* he suggests a fourfold community of being as the primary source of methodological constants:

> God and man, world and society form a primordial community of being. The community with its quarternarian structure is, and is not, a datum of human experience. It is a datum of experience in so far as it is known by man in virtue of his participation in the mystery of its being. It is not a datum of experience in so far as it is not given in the manner of an object of the external world, but is knowable only from the perspective of participation in it.[13]

One of Voegelin's main concerns is the loss of order, individual and social alike, that occurs when our deepest cultural symbols become divorced from primal experience through neglect of any of the primary community's four members. Thus, a truly atheistic symbolization or representation of reality generates a faulty world view and faulty women and men. So too with symbolizations that slight nature, society, or the self. Further, even adequate symbolizations that do justice to all four members can slide toward disorder if people lose the experiences that give the members their resonance, their three-dimensionality, their organic connection. A prime instance of this, in Voegelin's view, was the degeneration of philosophy, and later theology, into "doctrine," into treating God, man, nature, and grace as though they were independent objects of propositional discourse. This was a major factor in modernity's loss of reality, because it alienated many who sought a living, experiential truth and God.

The fourfold primal community of being is constant. It was the epochal achievement of the prophets and philosophers to discover or differentiate it and so create the "ecumenic" age, the horizon of universal, worldwide humanity. A return to the core experiences that make humanity ecumenic is the means to health which Voegelin seeks.

> In our time, the inherited symbolisms of ecumenic humanity are disintegrating, because the deforming doctrinalization has become socially stronger than the experiential insights it was originally meant to protect. The return from symbols which have lost their meaning to the experiences which constitute meaning is so generally recognizable as the problem of the present that specific references are unnecessary. The great obstacle to this return is the massive block of accumulated symbols, secondary and tertiary, which eclipses the reality of man's existence in the Metaxy. To raise this obstacle and its structure into consciousness, and by its removal to help in the return to the truth of reality as it reveals itself in history, has become the purpose of *Order and History*.[14]

The "metaxy" is Plato's "in-between," the proper span of human consciousness, which in health ranges between the divine Mind above and the Unbounded *(apeiron)* below. In the metaxy, human consciousness discovers itself in tension toward the divine ground of its being. Moved by God, we experience an anxiety, an existential questioning, because we realize we are not our own origin and destiny. This questing movement, or *zētēsis,* shows God experientially present as the known unknown, the goal of our awareness. "God" is the intelligibility, the adequate reason, the sufficient causality we instinctively ask to make sense of ourselves and of the world. The great advantage of Voegelin's sketch of the primordial community of being, the basic polarities of reality, is its close ties to living experience.[15]

Eric Voegelin's usefulness for us here is to provide the categories of nature, society, self, and God as the structure of our survey of recent theological literature. This structure assures our giving each primal member of reality its due. It gives us as well the beginnings of a critical principle in that any theology which fails to consider a primal member of reality, or fails to correlate all the members, must be inadequate. Finally, the close ties between this fourfold structure and the basic religious experiences of seeking and finding God should keep our survey experiential. If "communications" is to succeed, it has to evoke experiences that auditors can recognize. Since all who read this are themselves polar to nature, society, and God, I hope that Voegelin's categorization will help to make the individual surveys of which this book is comprised relevant for the ecological, political, personal, and religious zones of their lives.

The four primal partners to the community of being are ecumenical, in the sense that the prophetic and philosophic experiences in which they became clear showed them to be universal, true for everyone, and of the essence of "humanity." This book, insofar as it deals with Christian theology, cannot be completely universal. Jesus is a contingent, free, historical event. However much a high Christology of the sort espoused here finally holds Christ to be a universal Logos ingredient in humanity's very constitution, it remains that we have such a Christology only in the fact of Jesus' life, death, and resurrection. Nonetheless, no Christian theology descriptive of recent trends or prescriptive of future imperatives will go far if it fails to grant Jesus a structural place at least equal to that of nature, society, self, and God. Christians find salvation in Jesus' name and no other. Christian theologians are unfaithful to the source "Christian texts" and perhaps also to the source "common human experience and language," if they do not make Jesus the center, the pivot, or even the "scandalous" moment that identifies Christian faith through history. As Hans Küng says, what makes Christian faith distinctive is precisely Jesus. Consequently, "Jesus" becomes for us here a fifth category.

A BRIEF PREVIEW

Let us allow the five following examples to serve as some illustration of what we may hope to achieve here:

In *Process Theology,* John Cobb and David Griffin treat under the heading "The Global Crisis and a Theology of Survival" what they call "the spatio-temporal scale," "the human and the natural," "ecological sensitivity," and "responsibility and hope." Under "ecological sensitivity" they write:

Process theology calls for still further extension of the sense of participation. The whole of nature participates in us and we in it. We are diminished not only by the misery of the Indian peasant but also by the slaughter of whales and porpoises, and even by the "harvesting" of the giant redwoods. We are diminished still more when the imposition of temperate-zone technology onto tropical agriculture turns grasslands into deserts that will support neither human nor animal life.[16]

Positively, process thought is at work here showing how intrinsic nature is to human beings, how vital whales, porpoises, redwoods, and even more so Indian peasants, are to our understandings of how things are and what they call us to do. Negatively, because it is not clear that the Bible is more important for these authors than their philosophical sources, one might reasonably doubt that their world is compatible with those of Paul, John, and the authors of Genesis. Nonetheless, it is a very stimulating world, because in it nature has such rich religious import. The 1980s need such reflection, such calls to realize nature's holiness.

A second example concerns society. Phillip Berryman quotes the following from a manifesto by six Brazilian Catholic bishops:

Capitalism must be overcome. It is the great wrong, the cumulative sin, the rotten root, the tree that bears the fruit we know: poverty, hunger, sickness, and death to the great majority. For this reason the system of ownership of the means of production (of factories, of land, of commerce, of banks, of credit sources) must be overcome. . . . We want a world in which the fruits of labor are shared by everyone. We want a world in which one works not to get rich but to provide everyone with the necessities of life: food, health, a house, education, clothing, shoes, water, and light. We want

a world in which money will be at the service of men,
and not man at the service of money.[17]

Clearly, the bishops have forged a provocative combination of Marx and the Bible. Joining socioeconomic criticism
and evangelical utopianism, they condemn the present Brazilian social order and prophesy for the future. The
bishops' message is that it is sinful, deeply and grossly so,
to thwart justice and condemn millions of human beings
to grinding poverty. It remains to be seen how liberation
will fare after CELAM III, the most recent meeting of the
Latin-American bishops, but few Latin-American theologians countenance the existing social order and all are
caught in an ancient struggle of how not to render to
Caesar the things that are God's. Society raises questions
of culture, mythology, politics, but its deepest issue is justice. So, as sociology has had greater impact, justice has
come more to the theological fore.

Third, the self, obviously, is a social being, so justice and
injustice greatly shape its story. The self is impoverished
if it does not commune with nature, and if it does not deal
with nature reverently it is vicious and destructive. Still,
the self is not reducible to its social or natural relation-
ships. Each self is a pilgrim toward death and the mystery
of God. Each person suffers and enacts a unique story, an
unrepeatable drama of time. Speaking of the failure that
can mark that drama, Penelope Washbourn writes:

The end of my marriage shattered my growing sense
of complacency and pride at my own success. I was
unmasked and that prideful girl was no more. Gradually, from the silence of the months of pain I began to
talk to friends that I had cut off from seeing my an-
guish. At first I heard only my self-pity as I told the
story of the failure of my hope. Gradually the immedi-
ate grief faded and I began to rebuild. . . . Maybe

nothing has been more productive of growth in my-
self than what I initially experienced as death.[18]

As this description testifies, the self's journey can be
painful; more often than not, we are forced to ascend Mt.
Carmel. Ironically enough, our time is also experiencing a
return to classical asceticism. Recent literature makes
clear our pressing need for stable verities. Among them
are that we die, that we are born ignorant and do well not
to lose ground, and that no society has achieved the justice
and love on which our hearts are set.

Some of our contemporaries find a practical return to
such verities in the instructions for meditation of Shunryu
Suzuki and Yasutani Roshi. In them they find Buddhist
selflessness and the capacity for living in the present. Others look to traditional Western masters. Either way, serious analysis of the self today spotlights contemplation. In
Greek terms, it calls us back to the injunction to "know
thyself." In evangelical terms, it revives Jesus' word that
his branches must be pruned.

Fourth, the wonders of nature, social problems, and the
self's longings for peace all press toward the limit questions of religion proper; they raise the issue of "God."
Lately, our culture seems again to appreciate this, and the
Lord of History, not long ago pronounced dead, has been
making a comeback. This may have been predictable. Voegelin sardonically says, "Man cannot live by perversion
alone," and it is remarkable that much secular disavowal
of God now rings rather hollow. We hear it as an option,
a "position," not an argument, and it usually misses the
real significance of "God," as Karl Rahner puts it:

> The real word "God" is not simply identical with the
> word "God" which appears in a dictionary lost among
> thousands and thousands of other words. For this dic-

tionary word "God" only represents the real word
which becomes present for us from out of the wordless texture of all words through their context and
through their unity and totality, which itself exists and
is present for us. This real word confronts us with
ourselves and with reality as a whole, at least as a
question. . . . Its demise can be thought of only along
with the death of man himself.[19]

Rahner's thesis is that all theology is anthropology,
that we approach God through the meaning of being
human. In Karl Jaspers' terms, the word "God" is
poised on the *boundary,* pointing to the mystery into
which all sustained reflection leads. Rahner's predilection is for the awareness of God that comes from grasp-
ing the human spirit's anticipations and grounds, its so-
called transcendental aspects, his legacy from German
idealism.

Liberation theologians agree with Rahner's theology,
but insist on action. Their God is that of Abraham, Isaac,
Jacob, and Jesus. He takes sides, accusing evildoers and
fighting on behalf of those who suffer evil. Paraphrasing
Marx, the liberationists say that while in the past the task
of theology was to understand the world through revelation, today the task of theology is to change it.

These four examples indicate major recent movements,
but Jesus remains the central focus for a genuinely Christian theology. Lately Christology has returned to basic
issues and particularly to the historical Jesus. There, many
claim, lie Christianity's origins, axis, and future self-understanding. Hans Küng, for one, locates these origins in such
questions as:

How did this condemned, heretical teacher become
Israel's Messiah, the Christ? How did this disowned

prophet become "Lord," how did this unmasked se-
ducer of the people become "Saviour," this rejected
blasphemer "God's Son"? After leaving this man to
die in complete isolation, how did it come about that
his followers not only clung to his message under the
impact of his "personality," his words and deeds, not
only summoned up their courage some time after the
catastrophe to continue to proclaim his message of the
Kingdom and the will of God—for instance, the "Ser-
mon on the Mount"—but immediately made this person himself the essential content of the message?[20]

To answer these questions, one must pass through hermeneutics to the world of biblical reality, and it is encouraging that recent biblical interpretation has sought
the assistance of philosophers such as Paul Ricoeur to accomplish this. Though some exegetes are trapped by struc-
turalism, as many of their teachers were trapped by
philology, others are moving to a new level of self-criticism. Their work promises a new Christ of hope and liberation.

CHAPTER 2

Nature
and the Ecological Crisis

RECENT THEOLOGIES OF NATURE

In 1972 Joseph Sittler tried in *Essays on Nature and Grace*[1] to situate "grace," the forces of God's revealed love, in what he called "the web of nature." To do so he first traced the history of the doctrine of grace in recent ecumenical and American theology and explored the rich significance of grace in Scripture. Then, returning to an ecumenical context, he expounded some neglected themes of the Eastern fathers, preserved by Orthodoxy, including the notion of the *pantokrator,* the Logos as Lord and ruler of physical creation.

This Eastern physicalism contrasted historically with a Western tendency, beginning with Augustine, to treat grace as a medication for human sinfulness. From the Reformation to the present the West has suffered from this, finding itself largely without a sufficiently physical, organic conception of grace to correspond to nature as recast by modern science. If we are to recover an adequate conception of grace, Sittler argues, we must rethink the basic question and mystery of physical things as they are, moving with the creative scientist and artist toward the mood of poet Richard Wilbur's line, "Guard and gild what's common, and forget uses and prices and names; have objects speak."[2]

When objects speak, the world revives and the ecological web as well. For Sittler, this is a matter of survival, of what is necessary if things are to continue to exist, of what is essential to prevent the perversion or distortion of the given nature that things have.

The grace of nature, then, shows in what makes for nature's preservation, beauty, and life. We find the forces of God's creative care when we share the world gracefully with all things, letting them be, in their brightness and beauty. Sittler's theology of creation is essentially aesthetic. Grace comes to nature because God cannot despise anything made. We discover this grace, appreciate it, and cooperate with it by living ecologically, in the context of nature's web.

Thus, one of the concerns of theology of nature recently is to sharpen our religious instincts, our sensitivity to the goodness of creation. In a study representing more analytic concerns, John J. Compton has probed how we ought to conceive God's action in nature. For many scientists, divine agency is unthinkable, since they accept "the apparent impossibility of any divine action in a completely causal nature order." But if we conceive divine action by analogy with human action, divine action may become quite possible: "Just as human bodily movement is or may be causally conditioned in its physical linkage, although remaining an intentional action with full meaning, so also a causally determined cosmic history may be an expressive action of God." In other words, to act in the world God does not have to find a gap in its chemistry or physiology. If we do not force God to be self-complete, absolutely self-controlling, as much past theism did, divine action can mean "just the sort of dynamic, creative, novelty-produc-

ing evolution that takes place."[3] If so, what nature is up to
is precisely creation. Compton's essay involves a recon-
ception of "God" and divine action based on current scientific views of natural causality and evolution. The hints he
gives are especially those of process theology.

Daniel Day Williams' essay "Changing Concepts of Nature" begins historically, tracing the changes that our conception of nature has undergone from classical times to
modern, and concludes with a discussion of the recent
concept of "possibility." Possibility is indeterminate. It implies that the future is truly open. Further, it means that
the human community has a political relation to nature,
because if evolution is indeterminate, we must in part
decide what nature will be in the future. In other words,
since today natural history cannot be separated from
human history, natural history's possibility forces us to
reassess what we should expect in time. How political and
theological this becomes is clear in the questions that Williams raises:

> Can man achieve productivity, a community of peace,
> and the release of his creative powers? If we are to
> avoid disaster, the movement of human life must be
> toward a *polis* of humanity. We cannot expect Kenya
> to preserve its marvelous richness of wildlife unless
> the international community is willing to share the
> financial cost. We cannot deal with the population
> explosion in some countries and not in others. Control
> of the drug traffic is an international problem. The
> development of food production requires the cooper-
> ation of government, business, and science on a
> worldwide scale. World order under law is the only
> final alternative to suicidal warfare. We are led back
> to the profundity of the biblical view of history and
> the hope for the Kingdom of God as a *society of all*
> under God.[4]

In Williams' view, an up-to-date theology of nature would stress God's immanence: "God is not another name for evolution, or nature, or process, but he is the creative spirit and the ultimate order that makes process possible and order intelligible."[5] To those who fear that this immanence would destroy God's transcendence and so produce a divinity less than divine, Williams replies that "God" should retain at least three significances that protect divine sovereignty: (1) God remains the power of being, who alone determines that a world should exist, alone sustains it in being, and alone interacts with it totally; (2) God is unchanging, everlasting, and alone carries along the whole realm of possibility: (3) God's goodness includes all possible goods, and it labors through its integrity for the fulfillment in creative harmony of the whole "society" of beings.

Compton and Williams tie the evolutionary world more closely to divinity than classical theologians did. As modern thinkers, aware of nature's vast dynamism in a way that classical theologians could not be, they insist that a God uninvolved in real time, not interacting with evolution, is pale, irrelevant, unworthy of contemporary awe. It is clear that Sittler would share this. It is clear as well that all three thinkers derive their theology of nature from process thought, which regards God as limited. Can a limited God ground the hope that evolution and history require?

Williams is aware of this question, as his efforts to preserve divine transcendence indicate. His fellow process theologians have been equally astute. So strong is this school's commitment to God's interaction with the world, though, that it is willing to qualify divine sovereignty. John B. Cobb, Jr., and David Griffin, for instance, make God's interaction one of the prime theses of their *Process Theol-*

ogy: An Introductory Exposition, confessing in the fore-
word that they reject a great deal implied by the word
"God" in the Christian past. For them, God is not a law-
giver, a judge, an unchanging or passionless absolute, the
world's controlling power, a sanctioner of the status quo,
or, for that matter, male.[6]

For Cobb and Griffin, divinity is "Creative-Responsive
Love," a biblicized updating of Whitehead's expression
"dipolar deity."[7] The implications of this are considerable
for the theology of nature. First, Creative-Responsive
Love makes more sense in an evolutionary framework
than the classical Christian deity does: if God's influence
is persuasive rather than controlling, if the world is ordered through divine "lure" rather than blueprinted from
the beginning, then evolution is necessary, something God
could not have accomplished more efficiently in a twin-
kling.

Second, if God is not the absolute controlling power, the
problems of theodicy, of whether God can be called just
although the world is evil, greatly diminish. There are
things out of God's hands, and there are limits to God's
dominion, and, consequently, to God's responsibility. As a
result, theodicy becomes a matter of estimating whether
the overall venture of creation is worth its pains:

> Hence, the question as to whether God is indictable
> for the world's evil reduces to the question as to
> whether the positive values enjoyed by the higher
> forms of actuality are worth the risk of the negative
> values, the sufferings.[8]

Third, Cobb and Griffin argue that God's purpose in
evolutionary development is to maximize beauty and enjoyment. All creatures have some capacity for enjoyment.
This obviously is graduated, but it is real because every

existent, from molecule to mammal, has what Teilhard de Chardin called a "within." All existents are fellows, all have a claim on our respect and on our concern for their beauty and well-being. All beings in nature have rights, and we break a sacred law when we fail to accord these to them.

But can the process God ensure that history will secure these rights, that evolution will succeed? Cobb and Griffin answer forthrightly:

> Process theism . . . cannot provide the assurance that God's will is always done. It does affirm that, no matter how great the evil in the world, God acts persuasively upon the wreckage to bring from it whatever good is possible. It asserts that this persuasive power with its infinite persistence is in fact the greatest of all powers. But it does not find in that assertion assurance that any particular evil, including the evil of the imminent self-destruction of the human race, can be ruled out.[9]

This means that the future is truly open, that what we do with human liberty will determine earthly creation's fate.

This may not, of course, be identical with a New Testament faith that Christ has overcome the world, that God will wipe every tear from our eyes. Lewis Ford, whose process theology deals more directly with biblical convictions than does that of Cobb and Griffin, is as forthright as they in admitting process theology's dilemma:

> If the good triumphs no matter what, the sufferings that God allows us to endure on the way lose their meaning because he could have accomplished his purposes without them. Yet . . . all the hopes and strivings of man are unmasked as utter vanity if the end of the universe is simply a wasting away into nothingness.[10]

Relying upon Whitehead's notion of "peace," Ford suggests that individual immortality and direct compensation for innocent suffering are a "restless egotism" we can well do without. On the issue of cosmic theodicy, he sets the issue as starkly as Cobb and Griffin:

> Either God has the power to overcome evil unilaterally, and he should have already, *or* he does not, and we have no guarantee that he will ever be able to. Process theism has chosen to embrace the second horn of this dilemma. God cannot guarantee that evil will be overcome simply because he is not the sole agent determining the outcome of the world.[11]

Ford goes on to make a case for the likelihood of God's persuasive triumph, but ultimately he cannot echo the biblical assurance that all will be well. This suggests that *(a)* the disjunction which Ford poses is not absolute, in that God could have the power to overcome evil unilaterally and legitimately not have done so "already," *(b)* the resurrection is an obvious counterexample, and *(c)* process theology must grapple more deeply with the mysteries of the creator-creature relationship. For example, it must deal with Karl Rahner's claim that human freedom increases in direct proportion to our closeness to God, that true human freedom serves a quite definite plan of the creator. In that case, the notion of divine transcendence controls theological imagination and governs descriptions of God's actions more successfully than process theology can.

SCIENCE AND RELIGION

Most theology of nature has to contend as a central methodological issue with the relationship between the procedures of the physical sciences which take nature as their peculiar province and the procedures by which theology presumes to say something about nature that the sciences cannot.

It is commonly conceded that the Christian doctrine of creation and Christian theology's confidence in nature's intelligibility have historically been major sponsors of the scientific enterprise, as Robin Attfield's recent study, "Science and Creation," suggests. Frederick Ferré has also dealt with the precise sorts of explanation that science and theology each pursue. He finds that scientific deduction does not cover all of scientific explanation, since clarifications of it frequently take the form of theory or paradigm revision. But these clarifications, if not arbitrarily curtailed, call for comprehensive ordering. This means that physical science has a legitimate, even natural bent toward metaphysics. Beyond the enterprise of explanation, however, there is ethical assessment, which becomes a matter of theology when reflection on the *purposes* of the natural systems generates worship. Only worship "may conceivably offer a way through which men can responsibly cope with the cognitive bottomlessness of the arbitrary."[12]

Reflecting on this movement from deduction to worship, Ferré proposes a criterion for the theological explanation of natural phenomena:

> First, is this proposed explanation in keeping with the best findings of the special sciences, whose explanatory models and theories lie at the beginning of the quest for understanding and may not be ignored without cognitive peril? Second, has the candidate for explanation overcome the disconnection of separate explanatory paradigms in the various special sciences by some coherent principle of theoretical unification

that is also adequately inclusive? And, finally, has the value dimension of human life been seriously considered and tested against humanity's most profound intuitions of ultimate worth?[13]

For Ferré, science, philosophy, and theology ought to form a continuous, mutually dependent sequence.

Ian Barbour, who edited the volume in which the Compton, Williams, and Ferré studies appeared, published shortly thereafter a full analysis of the comparisons between science and religion. Of scientific models Barbour writes:

> First, models have a wide variety of uses in science. They serve diverse functions, some practical and some theoretical. Second, theoretical models are novel mental constructions. They originate in a combination of analogy to the familiar and creative imagination in inventing the new. They are open-ended, extensible, and suggestive of new hypotheses. Third, such models are taken seriously but not literally. They are neither pictures of reality nor useful fictions; they are partial and inadequate ways of imagining what is not observable.[14]

In religion, models function in the interpretation of experience, the expression of similitudes, the evocation of disclosures, and the construction of metaphysical systems. Since the last two of these can be subsumed under the first, religious models are at bottom concerned with interpreting experience and expressing attitudes. In interpreting experience they are similar to scientific models in that they are analogical—may be extended to new situations and make sense as units in their own right; they are not taken literally, yet they are more than "useful fictions"; and they are "organizing images" for structuring and interpreting patterns of events in personal life and the world. On the other hand, by expressing attitudes religious models differ from scientific ones in that they serve noncognitive functions, they elicit more personal involvement, and they imply formal beliefs and doctrines less than scientific models imply scientific theories.

As highly imaginative modes of investigation, science and religion employ a similar human facility for model-making. However, they do this for somewhat different ends. Science fashions models to understand the world; religion wants not only to understand the world but also to correlate its understanding with certain feelings and actions. Applying his analysis to Christianity, Barbour argues that theologians have developed five models for God's relation to the world. The first four are absolute monarch to kingdom, clockmaker to clock, person to person in dialogue, and agent to agent's actions. The fifth model, which he prefers, comes from process thought, and is that of

> a society in which one member is pre-eminent but not absolute. The universe is pictured as a community of interacting beings, rather than as a monarchy, a machine, an interpersonal dialogue or a cosmic organism.[15]

On the basis of what we discussed above, we can see that this fifth model likely has the advantage of integrating divinity with evolutionary process. On the other hand, it may be hard-pressed to guarantee final success to that evolutionary process, since it entails a nonabsolute God who cannot issue a final amen.

Another distinguished writer on the relation between science and religion is Harold K. Schilling, who has emphasized the mystery that science and religion share.[16] For the nuclear physicist, the molecular biologist, or the astronomer, each new discovery raises more questions than it answers. Level upon level, nature shows itself complex, interconnected, and endlessly full of surprises. Today's science is a far cry from the mechanistic science of the nineteenth century, which thought it only a matter of time before mathematics could determine all of nature's complex interrelationships. The wonder of today's investigators Schilling finds cognate to the religious person's wonder before divine mystery. For him, mystery is not an absence of clear comprehension, but an awareness of the creative source of being. Interacting with the world, luring it forward into the divine fullness, his God not only is compatible with evolution, but is the meaning of evolution's patterns and its goodness. Therefore, science and religion need not be adversaries. They ought, rather, to be allies.

Although process theologians seem most interested in the relationship of science to religion, theologians of other persuasions have treated the topic as well. Wolfhart Pannenberg's massive *Theology and the Philosophy of Science*, for instance, brings historical and hermeneutical insights to bear on the interrelationships of the disciplines that deal with physical nature, human meaning, and God.

Insofar as Pannenberg's views are accessible, he seems to want to bridge the divide between the physical and the human sciences:

> The study of meaning cannot in itself be the private reserve of the human sciences and cannot justify a theoretical opposition between human and natural sciences. The uniqueness of the human sciences can be described only in terms of their special form of perception of this common object. This form is a concentration on the historical character of the formation of meaning, which is intimately connected with its mediation by individual perception of meaning.

This is directly relevant to theology in that "ever since proofs of the existence of God from nature have proved untenable, modern theology has connected the question of God with a theory of man." In other words, modern theology has found philosophy of science unfriendly and so "in recent times has tried to find a basis more or less exclusively in the idea of man's subjectivity and self-understanding."[17] The risk in this is to allow Christian belief in creation to atrophy and to make theology appear bent on a self-serving effort to shield the humanities and history from the methods of discovery that the natural sciences use.

Pannenberg's analysis is an effort to acknowledge the right of natural scientists to apply their methods to human phenomena. At the same time he insists that the human being is meaningful as an *individual* system that forms itself "by descriptively apprehending, as the basis of his personal identity, semantic networks which transcend his existence."[18] In other words, the validity of the methods of a natural scientist such as a behavioral psychologist is limited. Insofar as behavioral scientists ignore or deny the individuality of human beings as systems centered on linguistic meaning, their methods misunderstand human reality and cannot develop an adequate science of humankind.

Concerning theological science, Pannenberg's analysis begins more simply:

An examination of the various forms in which the self-understanding of theology has been embodied in the course of its history has led us to the conclusion that theology, as it appears in the history of Christian theology, can be adequately understood only as a science of God.

However, when we start to unfold precisely what "science of God" means, things become more complex. In dialectical, back-and-forth fashion, Pannenberg shows that "God" is more a problem and a thematic point of reference than a secure dogmatic possession for theology today. Since God is not present to human experience as one object among others, we must assume that the reality of God is equally given for us to experience in other objects. This makes God's reality accessible to theological reflection only indirectly.[19]

Pannenberg develops this thesis with an admirable concern for experience as its basis:

> The reality of God is always present only in subjective anticipations of the totality of reality, in models of the totality of meaning presupposed in all particular experience. These models, however, are historic, which means that they are subject to confirmation or refutation by subsequent experience.[20]

From this central notion Pannenberg can proceed to a description of theological science in terms dear to the philosophy of science and of theology's internal organization in terms of its systematic, historical, exegetical, and practical tasks.

A rather different view of science and of the analytic philosophy derived from it appears in Stanley L. Jaki's 1974–1976 Gifford Lectures, published as *The Road of Science and the Ways to God*. In them, Jaki as a historian of science argues eruditely that physical science only developed in Christian culture because of that culture's realistic assumptions about the world's intelligibility.[21] The meaning of "only" in Jaki's argument is twofold. First, it was *only* Western Christian Europe that produced physical science as we know it. Neither Greece nor India nor

China, all of which had estimable art and philosophy, ever supported empirically based speculation sufficiently for a true science to become established. Second, when one ponders the historical uniqueness of Western science one finds, contrary to most current philosophies of science, that actual scientific practice presupposes a moderately realistic epistemology, or theory of knowledge. Part of this realistic epistemology is the belief that the world makes sense, is intelligible. But just as current history of science shows that Copernicus, Galileo, Newton, and the others of their stature had late-medieval forebears, so a sensitive analysis of the foundational constants in creative scientists' assumptions shows that they are derived from Christian notions of creation and contingency.

The biblical world view of Christian faith separated divinity and nature as creator and creature. This allowed the world to be both intelligible and singular. If the world is "created" in the strict sense, it comes by the free, rational choice of sovereign power and so is eminently reasoned and intended. Similarly, if the world is created, it is contingent, particular, and singular. Observing the world's particularity, its property of being here and now, scientists are interested to uncover what it actually, concretely is. Confident that the world is ordered, that this manifests reason, scientists never doubt that their labors can bear fruit. Consequently, all major scientists are in their *practice* moderate realists: creative intelligences who both attend closely to empirical singularity and speculate boldly about the patterns and laws of natural data. Copernicus, Newton, Einstein, and Planck all confess a moderate realism by their practice. Contrary to Bacon, Hume, Descartes, and Kant, to positivists and operationalists, creative science as actually practiced expresses human reason and intends a natural world exactly like that of Christian theology.

Jaki's Gifford Lectures are a reading in natural theology. On the basis of what creative scientists have de facto assumed about the world, he finds science a very compatible way to God. Like a latticework, science and theology mutually support each other. From the world's singularity and intelligibility, they build toward a divine first cause. Christian revelation can clarify some of the reasons—for instance, sin—why moderate realism is hard to maintain, and some of the implications of the world's singularity—for instance, its creation from nothing. But if we see science correctly through its history and epistemology, it leads us to theology.

A last specimen of recent reflection on the relationship betweenscience and religion is the work of David Tracy, who finds the two enterprises compatible in terms of "limit-questions." These are issues that take us to the boundary of ordinary conception and language and point to the horizon or ground that lies beyond. In Tracy's own words: "At the limit of both the scientific and moral enterprises, there inevitably emerge questions to which a response properly described as religious is appropriate." When he surveys recent philosophy of science, Tracy in fact finds a consensus that there is a religious dimension within the scientific enterprise itself. To explicate this consensus he uses Lonergan's notion of "self-transcendence," in which the very dynamics of science take the scientist beyond an "experienced world of sensitive immediacy to an intelligently mediated and deliberately constituted world of meaning."[22] In other words, an honest inquirer must satisfy the mind's hunger to know what sense data *mean.* Lonergan calls this move from data to meaning "intellectual" self-transcendence. However, beyond intellectual self-transcendence there are rational and moral self-transcendence, because the mind wants to know whether its explanatory insights are realistic and what value they carry. Satisfying these wants entails rational and moral self-transcendence. Even this does not quiet consciousness, though, for our experiences of evil, of evolution's frailty, of the inability of human societies to sustain development—in a word, our experiences of negativity—raise the question of *ultimate* intelligibility, rationality, and value. This is the question of God, the postulate for religious self-transcendence and unrestricted love.

Tracy acknowledges that one can achieve religious transcendence, find the boundaries where science opens onto theology, through means other than Lonergan's transcendental method:

> Either Louis Dupré's Hegelian phenomenology or Alfred North Whitehead's process philosophy or Stephen Toulmin's linguistic analysis of the "limiting questions" in science all mediate a similar understanding.[23]

We move, then, from views of science and religion which stress their external compatibility as realms of discourse to those which find an internal coherence based on the dynamics of human consciousness itself. Clearly, external and internal are related, but the advantage of stressing the latter is its focus on creative understanding, science's concrete source. Further, those who have studied creative scientists have found them artistic and intuitive. Michael Polanyi, for instance, found that the crucial parts of scientists' understanding always remain tacit, and Jeremy Bernstein felt that Einstein was driven by the passionate and aesthetic conviction that God does not play dice.[24] When scientists and theologians can discuss their existential drives, and can correlate them with the models or paradigms they use, many of their ancient controversies simply crumble. Joined in a common desire to understand, they can find themselves allied against obscurantism. Indeed, as Schilling found, they can discover that both science and theology are faith commitments to human honesty and natural mystery.

Does this mean that all is quiet on the science and religion front? Not quite, for there are still religious obscurantists who would deny the scientist autonomy to investigate such physical phenomena as evolution and universal creation, and there are still proponents of scientism, the ideology that all reality must be explained in empirical terms. Nonetheless, by concentrating on creative understanding philosophers of science and theologians alike have begun a dialogue fair with prospect for mutual respect and a lessening of past enmities.

ECOLOGY:
FINITE RESOURCES AND THE HUMAN FUTURE

Among the problems grouped under "nature," those of ecology are especially acute. For many writers, this is *the* scientific issue, for it entails nothing less than global survival. Literature on ecology is enormous, though most of it is by biologists, economists, or policy analysts, not by theologians. We shall subdivide it so as to show (1) the complexity of the ecological crisis, (2) the religious factor in its history, and (3) the ethical choices under debate.

Complexity. To grasp the dimensions of the ecological crisis one need read only a few collections of studies. Those edited by Herman E. Daly, Ian Barbour, and the American Academy of Arts and Sciences each show the tangle of biophysical, economic, political, and moral considerations that ecology now creates.[25]

On the most basic level, as Nicholas Georgescu-Roegen

has shown, the economic process only transforms valuable resources into waste. That is, there is a material base, subject to definite constraints, which provides a biophysical anchor for economics. For Georgescu-Roegen this means that

> every time we produce a Cadillac, we do it at the cost of decreasing the number of human lives in the future. Economic development through industrial abundance may be a blessing for us now and for those who will be able to enjoy it in the near future, but it is definitely against the interest of the human species as a whole, if its interest is to have a lifespan as long as is compatible with its dowry of low entropy. In this paradox of economic development we can see the price man has to pay for the unique privilege of being able to go beyond the biological limits in his struggle for life.[26]

Along the same line, Preston Cloud has surveyed the state of our mineral resources, showing that these nonreplaceable parts of the energy base are precariously low. The future looks even worse. Of the twenty critical mineral resources that Cloud plots, only eleven (four for the United States) are presently in such supply that they will not be exhausted by the year 2000. Indeed, only eight (three for the United States) are likely to last until 2042. This is at the present rates of usage, with no adjustment for increased population or per capita use. The energy implications alone are gruesome. For instance, uranium 235, indispensable to nuclear power, is not likely to last until the year 2000. It is later than we think:

> The year 2042, by which time even current rates of consumption will have exhausted presently known recoverable reserves of perhaps half the world's now usable metals, is only as far from the present as the invention of the airplane and the discovery of radioac-

tivity. In the absence of real population control or catastrophe there could be fifteen billion people on earth by then![27]

Cloud admits that there are many unknowns in the energy crisis, not least our future population growth. Paul Ehrlich and John Hodern, however, have argued that five "theorems" describe the overall relationship of population to environment, and these are not encouraging:

1. Population growth causes a *disproportionate* negative impact on the environment.

2. Problems of population size and growth, resource utilization and depletion, and environmental deterioration must be considered jointly and on a global basis. In this context, population control is obviously not a panacea—it is necessary but not alone sufficient to see us through the crisis.

3. Population density is a poor measure of population pressure, and redistributing population would be a dangerous pseudosolution to the population problem.

4. "Environment" must be broadly construed to include such things as the physical environment of urban ghettos, the human behavioral environment, and the epidemiological environment.

5. Theoretical solutions to our problems often are not operational and sometimes are not solutions.

Ehrlich and Hodern conclude that

population control, the redirection of technology, the transition from open to closed resource cycles, the equitable distribution of opportunity and the ingredients of prosperity must *all* be accomplished if there is to be a future worth having.[28]

The contributors to Daly's volume think "steady-state" economy is the only solution to the ecological crisis. Utilizing sophisticated computer models, Jorgen

Randers and Donella Meadows have concluded that there are only about 3.2 billion hectares of arable land. At present productivity rates we need about 0.4 hectare to support each person. If the present level of productivity were doubled and population held steady, we would still run out of land about the year 2050. If productivity were quadrupled, the year would be 2075. The stark and simple conclusion Randers and Meadows reach summarizes the conviction of all the contributors: "Because our environment—the earth—is finite, growth of human population and industrialization cannot continue indefinitely. . . . In a limited world we cannot maximize everything for everyone."[29] Turning toward a steady-state economy regarding the depletion of nonrenewable resources is for many ecologists the scientific and moral crux of humanity's future.

To concretize this somewhat, let us consider the problem of world hunger. In a panel on food and population, Donella Meadows has discussed the three approaches to solving world hunger that politicians presently consider: population control, food distribution, and food production. Her own words show how we are doing, and where religion might assist:

> The problem seems serious enough to require every response we can think of. Of course disagreements will arise about how many resources we should be putting into each of these options. It is clear that worldwide we are putting most resources into raising more food, the technological solution. We give much less attention to redistributing the food, which is the ethical solution, and virtually none at all on a worldwide basis into doing something about population, the social solution. We hardly even know how to begin on that one. I would suggest the priorities should be just the reverse.[30]

Even those who are optimistic about future food production, who dispute the costs of chemical fertilizers, or who find nature more renewable than the prophets of exhaustion claim do not dispute that we have serious ecological and ethical problems. Many of them join in castigating our industrialists, who close their eyes to the ecological facts and push for an economy of maximum growth.[31]

An economist who castigates industrialists and consumers equally, and with a marvelously delicate touch, is Barbara Ward. Two things distinguish her recent *Progress for a Small Planet* and together make it perhaps the most useful of nontheological resources. First, it is comprehensive. Taking today's economic order as a series of globally interdependent systems, Ward describes the problems of both the industrial, developed nations and the agricultural, developing nations. Second, it is positive. Whether the issue be energy, food, urbanization, or employment, Ward supplies an encouraging array of instances where creative solutions are already in place. Concerning industrial recycling, for instance, she can report that

> opencast coal areas in West Germany have been restored not simply to previous but to higher standards of productivity. Land once stripped for mining can have its productivity restored by the judicious use of sewage sludge and composted refuse. In some areas, properly compacted wastes have been landscaped, reafforested, turned into hillsides and picnic areas— one thinks of the 150-foot Mount Trashmore (or Mount Hoy, to give it the official name), near Chicago, with its adjoining lakes made from abandoned gravel pits. Its success has prompted a new project in the Greene Valley, with two 250-foot hills for skiing and hiking.[32]

So too regarding the nations of the southern hemisphere, where these problems are absolutely critical. It is among the rural peoples of the southern hemisphere that 80 percent of the world's "absolute poverty" occurs in the forms of malnutrition, high mortality, crippling disease, illiteracy, and unemployment. Moreover, these same people have the highest birthrates, with the result that over 40 percent of the people in the world's rural areas are less than fifteen years old. It is from figures such as these that economists derive their predictions that by the year 2000 the earth will have 6 billion people, and that at least 1.5 billion of them will be unable to earn enough to live on. Nonetheless, despite the harrowing prospects which these figures raise, land reform such as that accomplished in Japan from Meiji times on, local production of combustible gas from human and animal wastes in India, mechanized irrigation developed in China, villagization programs in Tanzania, reforestation projects in Peru, and others show that developing peoples do occasionally turn things around.

The core problem is for the interconnected world nations to see the pervasive need for a conserving, humane attitude toward natural resources. Were such an attitude joined to a generous sense of justice (the Marshall Plan that revitalized Europe after World War II is Ward's favorite example), we would have a good chance to save our small planet, and to free its poor from their miseries. When people, even very "backward," downtrodden people, are given some control over their lives and their land, and are provided some concrete technical help, they can mount creativity and energy that often halve their problems. It is this creativity and energy that remain our most vital resource, and the lack of them remains the sharpest indicator that the world is awry.

To be sure, ecology is complex in that it is scientific, technological, economic, political, and ethical all in one. What strikes the religious observer, though, is that most failures of imagination and nerve in its regard are due to shortsightedness and introverted self-serving. In fact, ecological literature is a depressing initiation into human irrationality, for beneath the legitimate debates about what the statistics mean one regularly senses a will not to hear, a will to avoid the call to conversion.

The Religious Factor. Precisely because the ecological crisis spotlights the importance of basic attitudes, a lively subdebate has arisen about the historical sources of the Western tendency to ravage the land. A useful volume edited by David and Eileen Spring, *Ecology and Religion in History,* presents some of the sides to this debate.[33] The most celebrated statement, with which the volume begins, is Lynn White's "The Historical Roots of Our Ecological Crisis." White's thesis is that the Bible desacralized nature and made human beings think of themselves as overlords empowered to use nature as they would. In White's own words, "Formerly man had been part of nature; now he was the exploiter of nature." On the basis of their biblical commission, human beings felt free to develop technology (in farming, for instance) that dealt with the earth simply as raw material. Thus, northern European peasants developed a plow so heavy that it required eight oxen to pull it, and they were quite heedless that it brutally ripped the soil. Rather rhetorically White asks," Is it coincidence that modern technology, with its ruthlessness toward nature, has so largely been produced by descendents of those peasants of northern Europe?"

As one might expect, White's broad condemnation of Christian attitudes toward nature brought a quick response. James Barr, speaking for Scripture scholars, pointed out problems in White's reading of the Bible.[34] Less theological analysts, such as Lewis Moncrief, denied that religion alone shapes any society's ecological views.[35] Yi-Fu Tuan, a geographer with cross-cultural interests, underlined the oft-forgotten truth that a theology or set of social ideals may have only nominal impact on practice. And Chinese reverence for nature is itself a case in point. If one were to read only Chinese poetry and philosophy, East Asia could seem to be an ecological paradise. In fact, the Chinese have often abused their land. Deforestation, for instance, has been a perennial problem in China, creating both ugly landscapes and severe flooding.[36]

Extending Tuan's argument, René Dubos has pointed out that climate determines the conditions for solving many ecological problems.[37] This means that the same techniques practiced in two different places can devastate one and do the other little lasting damage. Thus, it was the bad luck of the Harappan, Mayan, Khmer, and Teotihuacán cultures to wear out their soil, though there is no proof that they were more brutal than other peoples, and though their culture was not shaped by the Bible.

Thus, the historical influence of religion on ecology is complex and debatable. Most commentators agree, however, that strongly anthropocentric attitudes have wrought the greatest havoc. Though the best Christian thought may not have sanctioned this attitude, many Westerners have in fact acted as though the world were their personal possession. Whether the best corrective would be reviving a sense of stewardship or returning to a pagan reverence for nature, it is clear that religion can have an important role in the ecological future, for much of what we choose to do about energy and food will depend on how we conceive the good life.

Ethical Choices. When ecological discussion turns from debates about resource depletion or population increase, it soon begins to examine the hard choices that lie ahead. Garrett Hardin has performed a useful function by writing grim scenarios for the results of inaction on, for instance, population control. True, there have been efforts at population control, but "the situation has grown much worse in the past 25 years. A quarter of a century ago about a billion and a half people were malnourished. After 25 years of progress, two and a half billion are malnourished."[38] By comparing the progress of India and China over this period, Hardin concludes that the best policy for affluent countries like America is probably only to make others help themselves.

Roger Shinn accepts Hardin's grim scenario but finds more room for American action:

> Barry Commoner and many others have pointed out, as Hardin himself did, how much higher our rate of consumption is than that of most of the world. The figures he cited on food were about three to one, and energy about ten to one. My students from other parts of the world say, "Such a little bit of retraction on your part could do so very much where we are."[39]

If we couple these consumption rates with data suggesting that birthrates fall only when affluence rises, we can see that only by bringing underdeveloped nations to relative sufficiency can we avert starvation. If redistributing the world's wealth would accomplish this, ethical persons have little choice but to promote redistributing.

Those ethical choices stalk us at every turn, for we cannot separate our own humanity, what Loren Eiseley called "the lethal factor," from nature's cycles. Humanity's role is not only one of agency in pollution and despoliation, it is also one of effect, in that human beings are starving and living in squalor, affected by our choices. Unfortunately, as Paul Santmire has noted, ecologists and others committed to social change often consider each other more as enemies than as allies.[40] This is tragically shortsighted on both sides. In terms of priority, Santmire agrees with the social changers: "Generally social justice must be given priority over survival in our theological hierarchy of values (here the way of the cross can be paradigmatic)." However, we cannot ignore "survival," for there will be no society at all unless we attack our very real environmental problems. The political theologians have tended to ignore these problems, because they consider them subissues of politics or economics. But there is simply too much hard scientific data on ecological damage to warrant this view. In any intelligent estimate, we must work for *both* social justice and ecological change. Precisely how to do this Santmire does not explain. It would seem to mean at the very least the sacrifice of some of the northern nations' affluence.[41]

A starting point for ecological and social issues is, in fact, distributive justice: are we being fair about the limited resources and wealth of a single ecosystem and world economy? If we accept that the goods of the earth are for all the earth's people, we must alter the distribution of those goods and address the real possibility that there will be only a spartan few of them in the future. If the recent workshop sponsored by the Alternative Theology Project is any indication, white Americans show little stomach for such change. At that workshop, which was green wood compared to main-line North American views, white participants talked more about their own oppression by big business than about the third world.[42]

CONCLUSIONS

The literature of ecological ethics shows that practical steps such as shifting to renewable sources of energy, especially solar, advancing the Green Revolution in food production, distributing present supplies justly, and reducing population all depend on conversions at the deepest levels of attitude. These seem the only solid way to turn the entire economic and technological system around. It follows that theologians concerned about the 1980s would do well to ponder how they might raise their readers' ecological consciousness and convert them to simpler, more conserving life-styles. Buddhist and Taoist views that cherish nature as a great spiritual treasure constitute perhaps the best religious resource for such work.

As William LaFleur has shown,[43] indigenous Shinto convictions pressed Japanese Buddhism to affirm that all animals, plants, and trees possess the buddha-nature. For the twelfth-century monk and poet Saigyo, nature was the privileged symbol of ultimate reality. Behind Saigyo's poetry lay a strain in Japanese thought in which nature was more buddha-like than human beings, because it did not have to strive for enlightenment. Of course, most Western admirers of Eastern naturalism do not penetrate Buddhist enlightenment theory. Nonetheless, they glimpse what Saigyo turned into exquisite poetry: namely, that there is a "perfection" in nature, a blessed unselfconsciousness, and that we must approximate it in ourselves if we are to find fulfillment and peace. Consulting nature, becoming lost in it or dwarfed by it, is a way of entering transhuman fullness.

For an impressive combination of Eastern religion and humane economics, E. F. Schumacher has become something of an ecological patron saint. His economics is steady-state, and his practical experience as head of the British Coal Board and consultant to third world countries gives it special relevance. By rather simple calculations "on the back of an envelope," Schumacher shows that we are devouring our nonrenewable resources at an alarming rate. Like Barbara Ward, he offers concrete models for new patterns that could turn things around. The Scott Bader Commonwealth, with which Schumacher was associated, is a working model of just arrangements between ownership and labor—a more than viable alternative to the boredom and inequity on which too many capitalistic ventures depend.[44]

The soul of Schumacher's program, though, is his deservedly famous essay, "Buddhist Economics." A single sentence renders its flavor:

> The Buddhist point of view takes the function of work to be at least threefold: to give a man a chance to utilise and develop his faculties; to enable him to overcome his egocenteredness by joining with other people in a common task; and to bring forth the goods and services needed for a becoming existence.

This directly opposes most Western theories, because it places people before production and profits, and, in fact, Buddhist simplicity is a direct antidote to the ugliness and waste that our Western complexity nurtures. As Schumacher describes it,

> Since consumption is merely a means to human well-being, the aim should be to obtain the maximum of well-being with the minimum of consumption. Thus, if the purpose of clothing is a certain amount of temperature control and an attractive appearance, the task is to attain this purpose with the smallest possible

effort, that is, with the smallest annual destruction of
cloth and with the help of designs that involve the
smallest possible input of toil. The less toil there is, the
more time and strength is left for artistic creativity. It
would be highly uneconomic, for instance, to go in for
complicated tailoring, like the modern west, when a
much more beautiful effect can be achieved by the
skilful draping of uncut material.[45]

Schumacher is a proponent of "Buddhist" economics
not because he has vowed himself to Gautama, but because he has observed that a country like Burma possesses many of the spiritual remedies we presently
need. He is aware that almost all religions believe in
simplicity and nonviolence, and that few would not
agree that work should be subservient to human wel-
fare. Consequently, the Buddhist character of his economics might as easily be worked out in evangelical or
biblical terms. Of real importance is his call for conversion to a new way to think and work. This is precisely
what religions should be offering.

In Christian tradition, the hard sayings, the calls for
conversion, are the paradoxical ways to peace. It takes
little religious sophistication to see that the ecological crisis is an opportunity to muster the courage and wit to
enter a new evolutionary era in which spiritual fulfillment
will predominate over material. Notionally, that is hardly
difficult. Education, art, and creative science require little
capital outlay, if we know their real nature. Love, friend-
ship, worship, and community make little demand on our
bank account. Theologians ought to challenge economists
and people in business to design systems that replace material consumption with spiritual fulfillment, that place
people over profits, service over status, contemplation
over busyness. Preachers ought to challenge the comfort-

able in their churches with Jesus' saying that it is easier for a camel to pass through the eye of a needle than for the rich to enter the Kingdom of God. In this way, theologians and preachers might well make an enormous contribution to the nature of religion in the 1980s.

CHAPTER 3

Society and Church

HISTORY AND CULTURE

Whether they agreed or disagreed with Arnold Toynbee's *A Study of History,* historians of the last generation had to contend with the scope and depth of its vision. For the theologian, Toynbee possesses also the virtue of an explicit concern with religion, which he saw as the soul of historical meaning.

Shortly before his death in 1975, Toynbee produced a summary statement entitled *Mankind and Mother Earth,*[1] nothing less than a narrative history of the world. Sad to say, war is the major motif that Toynbee discovers in the history of one civilization after another. In the ancient Near East, India, China, the Mediterranean, and the New World, tribe followed tribe through conquest and slaughter. Most of Toynbee's six hundred pages recount who displaced whom and by what more or less barbaric means. To be sure, there were long stretches of prehistory when hunters, gatherers, and early agriculturalists limited their depredations to small skirmishes. And, of course, there were efforts in the arts and there were leaps of the religious spirit. Nonetheless, since the time that a mature agriculture made city life possible, human beings have shown themselves unable to manage society. Their signal failure has been to create a politically effective religious vision of justice. Hence history has been rife with wars and rumors of wars and demands of the theologian nothing less than a way to salvation.

The *Times Atlas of World History,*[2] for which Toynbee was a principal consultant, displays this full story, mainly of wars, in vivid cartography. Humanity has spent all but one sixteenth of its history in a Lower Paleolithic cultural life of hunting and gathering. From seventy thousand to forty thousand years ago technological developments began which have continued to change human life. Two major moments in this technological development have been the Neolithic invention of agriculture and the industrial revolution. It was the surplus of wealth that these two made possible which led to the social injustice and war that stamp history, ancient and modern alike. Further, since earliest civilization, human beings have fashioned impersonal institutions to deal with life on its large social scale. However, neither the state nor any other of its companion institutions have ever been completely able to satisfy the human craving for *personal* dealings. Hence, "what has been needed for the last 5,000 years, and has been feasible technologically, though not politically, for the last hundred years, is a global body politic composed of cells on the scale of the Neolithic-Age village-community—a scale on which the participants could be personally acquainted with each other, while each of them would also be a citizen of the world-state." Finally, as a result of the industrial revolution human technology now places the entire planet in peril.[3]

History as Religion

Regardless of whether we agree with all of Toynbee's theories, he forces us to reflect on history as a whole. Technologically, human beings have been mastering the earth and filling it, but spiritually they have let greed lead them to injustice after injustice and war after war. Because of this, they have created a global crisis of starvation, poverty, and pollution. Surely a theology trying to relate the Christian revelation of God's salvific love to world history and current culture has come to terms with this.

The fourth volume of Eric Voegelin's *Order and History* is perhaps one of the most remarkable analyses of history presently available to the theologian. Voegelin's topic is the "ecumenic age," the time beginning with roughly Alexander the Great in the middle of the fourth century B.C., when humanity became distinctly aware of itself as a single race spread throughout the world. In a variety of ways, different religions and intellectual events were connected with this realization. Israelite prophets and Greek philosophers achieved the most dramatic insights, but Persians, Christians, Muslims, Hindus, Buddhists, and Chinese all spoke to the concerns of the coming age.[4]

The heart of this process, for Voegelin, was the discovery that to be human is to exist in tension toward a mysterious divine ground. The basic lure or conscious energy that distinguishes humanity is a learned ignorance in regard to God. Israelite revelation disclosed that a sovereign mystery beyond the world created the world and formed the human soul. Greek philosophy discovered that human intelligence moves between the heights of this God and the depths of unbounded matter. Equally, these two "leaps in being" advanced human self-understanding toward the defining insight that we participate in eternal being in time.

Formed in our spiritual core by openness to divinity, we must yet stay entrenched in our earthly origins. The mystery of God is the non-answer, whose contemplation alone can direct us through the humble responsibilities of our time. Only by openness to God's too bright light can we keep our balance, be both images of the trinity and friends of the earth. Because Voegelin ties theses such as these to their historical discovery in Israel and Greece, and because he exposes them with the experiential certainty of a mystical philosopher, they are far from platitudes but are rich, symbolic expressions of what we are when we really are ourselves. What we really are is a vocation from God. At the core, we are called to openness to preexistent divine light and love. History is essentially the story of our clarification of this vocation. Thus, history is *religion,* not in the diminished sense this word has borne since Cicero, but in the profound sense of time that occurs with consummate meaning in God.

The diagnostic virtue of Voegelin's analysis is precisely its criteria for balance or right order. Voegelin accepts the Platonic notion that the state *(polis)* is the individual writ large. Against Marxists and positivists, he refuses to let the state either take precedence over individual human beings or demote them to the status of constituent atoms. The only concrete consciousness is that of individuals. The only effective political order is one that first honors the balance which human consciousness has by vocation and second persuades its citizens to embody justice.

History has misfired whenever ruling powers have either missed the balance of right order or have been unable to persuade their people to live by it. Current culture is misfiring in the same way. By closing themselves to God the secularist creators of current culture stray from right order. For individuals, this can bring only sadness, and by

and large individuals in our culture are deprived of the joy
that only comes from fulfilling one's inmost vocation. For
nations and the global community the current disorder
brings totalitarian bloodlust and selfish materialism. Either way leads to an injustice that wastes the lives of bil-
lions and an explosive violence that no state can contain.

History as Christian

Though Eric Voegelin frequently deals with Christian
materials, and though he well appreciates how Christianity synthesized Israelite revelation and Greek philosophy,
his is not a professedly Christian interpretation of history.
Langdon Gilkey's *Reaping the Whirlwind* is such an interpretation.[5]

Gilkey concerns himself at the outset with historicity,
the way that being in time is ingredient in human consciousness. Under analysis, history shows itself to be a po-
larity of destiny (determination) and freedom (human
choice), but finally mysterious, and thus having true sacral-
ity. Undergirding politics and daily affairs is an ultimacy
that envelopes them in holiness. Commentators who over-
look this ultimacy denature the historical process. Thus,
for Gilkey both the optimistic futurology of Herman Kahn
and the pessimist futurology of Robert Heilbroner are
wrong.

A center section on method serves to connect this description of modern historical consciousness to a revised
Christian doctrine of providence that emerges later in the
book. Principally, it is an effort to place Gilkey's own theology in the current context of hermeneutical sensitivity.

Part III of the book opens with a survey of traditional
notions of providence from Augustine and Calvin, pro-
ceeding to an analysis of modern views on the subject,
both theological and otherwise. Gilkey finds the tradi-

tional notions lacking in concern for the meaning of the historical process itself. What he demands of a modern theory is a balanced interpretation of all the principal ingredients: private and social forces, sin and grace, past, present, and future dimensions. In the final portion of the book Gilkey attempts to meet his own demand to so explain history that both secondary causes and God's primary causality receive their due.

In effect, Gilkey's construction is an adaptation of the Whiteheadean metaphysics in which God retains creativity and providence is "the universal divine activity of the preservation and continuity of creaturely being over time, as the ground of self-actualizing freedom and as the creative source of new possibilities in each situation."[6] Specifically, in Gilkey's conception of God divinity limits itself regarding creatures so as to leave them free, God's own power of being participates in history's passage, and the divine life accounts for both actual and possible being.

Compared to Voegelin's analysis of history, Gilkey's is distinctively theological in accepting the responsibility to clarify a doctrine of *providence.* Through time, believers hold, the Christian God's purposes are accomplished. Unlike Voegelin, Gilkey does not bring his analysis down to the concrete level of events. And unlike Karl Rahner, who, as we shall see below, makes Christ the center of evolutionary history, he does not pay much attention to the incarnation. Thus, Gilkey's discussion remains as much metaphysics as theology.

An interesting teller of the Christian story, whose work incidentally says a great deal about the current state of church history, is William A. Clebsch. *Christianity in European History,* his most recent work, distances itself from the faith commitments of the traditional church historian by trying to produce a humanistic account that makes sense of "the mutually dependent relation between the Christian religion and European culture by illustrating how the culture has been religiously shaped and how the religion, including its deity and savior, has been culturally conditioned."[7] To do this, Clebsch selects typical ways of being Christian in European history. The result is a challenging interpretation that focuses European Christian experience around five models.

During the period from 27 B.C. to A.D. 476, the principal "types," Clebsch finds, were martyrs and monks. They represent different reactions to the same dominant cultural question of how to be a faithful Christian as a Roman citizen. From 476 to 962 the context was comprised of chaotic conditions of the Germanic kingdoms. In response, Christian thought gravitated toward the problem of theodicy (God's justice), while Christian life organized itself around the prelates, especially the popes, who welded crozier to crown. The Holy Roman Empire is Clebsch's symbol for the cultural context of the years 962 to 1556. Its typical religious personalities were mystics like Bernard of Clairvaux and theologians like Anselm of Canterbury.

Moralists (e.g., Jeremy Taylor) and pietists (e.g., Nikolaus von Zinzendorf) dominated the years 1556 to 1806, when the cultural issue was allegiance to one's local portion of the Christian body. The modern period, 1806 to 1945, was dominated by activists like Dietrich Bonhoeffer and apologists like John Henry Newman. In Clebsch's view, the central political event to which they responded was the new nationalism, while the central religious phenomenon with which they grappled was the autonomy of modern consciousness, epitomized in the Enlightenment.

At the conclusion of his analysis of the modern period,

Clebsch says: "Put very simply, Europeans singly and collectively became their own do-it-yourself deities. But because their culture, tradition, and language were Christian in form, they specifically became do-it-yourself christs." This illumines our current religious situation, insofar as "autonomous European humanity assimilated the divine function of the Christian deity only to find it could not eliminate what it had devoured. Thus, the current term, 'post-Christian,' expresses a longing more than it describes an achievement. More accurate may be 'ex-Christian,' understood in apposition to 'ex-lover.' "[8]

Culture

Whether we take Gilkey's theological analysis of history, or Clebsch's humanistic one, we find that Western history significantly conjoins two thousand years of its experience to the Christian religion. Harkening to Clebsch's descriptions of modern autonomy and ex-Christianity, we may listen with a keener ear to analysts of current American culture. For Clebsch's descriptions are more than plausible. Efforts at self-salvation, proclamations that humanity has "come of age," introspection that constricts "reality" to what the self assumes, these mark much recent humanity, especially much recent intellectualism. Insofar as such "autonomy" suffers disorder, it supports the older, believing view that we are creatures rather than Gods, not at all autonomous. Our cultural problem is, therefore, discovering theonomy, the law that God gives within.

Perhaps it epitomizes Christian theology's current challenge that many find the received wisdom something to be assessed very critically. Robert Coles is one such. He is a writer, an artist, and, more than that, he is a psychiatrist, a physician of the spirit. That in itself need not make him independent. Many of his fellow psychiatrists are dog-

matic indeed. But Coles has traveled America for twenty
years listening to people whom most of his colleagues
never see. Above all, he has visited poor children in their
own homes. First it was black children in the South. Then
it was migrants, sharecroppers, and mountaineers. Third
it was black children in the North. Then it was Eskimos,
Chicanos, and Indians. Last it was rich children, the privileged ones.

The five volumes of The Children of Crisis are so many
windows on the subcultural worlds that millions of American children, and their families, inhabit. In them, middle-
class whites are rarely seen. What emerges is a profound
challenge to the wisdom of our stereotypes. Again and
again, Coles's children defeat our assumptions by insisting
on being themselves. Coles finds little in what he sees to
despise. To be sure, there is the "system" that consigns
most of his subjects to poverty and neglect. Nonetheless,
even within this vicious system, individuals live lives of wit
and grace. The tactile quality of Coles's prose renders
these individuals almost palpable. In them, "history" and
"culture" are more confounding and mysterious than
many theologians can hope to realize.

The concluding volume of Coles's series, *Privileged
Ones,* arose from the suggestions of poor people. "If
you want to know what's going on with us," they said,
"talk to them"—the whites, the mine owners, the big
farmers. So he did. The result is another turn of the
screw, for the children of the affluent, those who will
control most of tomorrow, are being carefully schooled
to retain the privileges they enjoy today. This is sum-
marized by a sketch of one child born to great wealth
in New Orleans. "She is today well on her way to being
a member of upper-crust, conservative New Orleans society, a perfect foil for a person like me, I suppose: the

preoccupation with dinner parties, flowers, dances, and clothes, not to mention a suitable suitor." Yet when she was eight, this girl used to look for hours on end out of her window at a cemetery wondering about the people buried there. "She would smile when she looked out and caught sight of an especially ornate, imposing, assertive monument of stone. She would, in her own way, meditate about life's meaning."[9]

But the girl made the mistake of telling her parents about this and worrying them to such an extent that they called a doctor. "The girl was implicitly and sometimes directly told to get on with it—life. She was, her parents decided, 'a little too introverted.' She had best be made 'busy.' They knew the enemy—inwardness."[10] Indeed, when the girl's grandmother died, her parents refused to let her see the corpse. Nor would they bury the grandmother in the cemetery across the street. By contrast, the black maid in the house, who was close to the little girl, argued that she ought to say good-by to her grandmother, as a way to sustain their relationship. The maid argued in vain.

This maid provides the conclusion to the book. She tells Coles that she tries to keep sight of "the end of things." From that perspective she finds that it is the white man, Mr. Charley, who is "the sad one." And, very soon, Mr. Charley's daughter will be like himself. "She wonders about life, and what it's about, and what the end of things will be. That's good. But she's stopping now, that's what they want: no looking, no staring, no peeking at life. No questions; they don't want questions. They go to a church a couple of times a year, Christmas and Easter, and no one asks them any questions there. No one asks them questions anyplace they go."[11] How much current American culture is described by this statement.

ECCLESIOLOGICAL ISSUES

A good example of contemporary ecclesiology is Avery
Dulles' recent study, "Jus Divinum as Ecumenical Problem."[12] Its focus is the current ecumenical discussion of
divine right or law, of what God entrusts to the church
irrevocably for safekeeping and transmission. After
sketching representative views from the time of the Reformation, Dulles surveys the opinions of leading theologians today. From this he fashions a series of "speculative
considerations" that express his own position. As is typical
of his work, they are admirably judicious.

Dulles begins by reflecting on the fundamental nature
of the church: "By very definition the Church is, under
Christ, the universal sacrament of salvation or, in other
words, the sacrament of Christ in the world."[13] From this
it follows that the church's obligation is to be the lasting
embodiment of the redemptive love which God showed in
Christ, and that the traditional four "notes" of the church
are unity, holiness, catholicity, and apostolicity. Further,
the unchangeable aspects of the church have a relational
character. They reach from a stable reference point in
Jesus Christ to the changing cultures of the people the
church would love.

Neo-Lutheran theology has especially spotlighted those
things which God has entrusted irrevocably to the church:
apostolic ministry, the rite of baptism, the meal that com-
memorates Jesus' Last Supper, and the sacramental showing of God's forgiveness. These are recorded in the New
Testament, and they flow from the basic mission of the
church to which the New Testament witnesses. At what
Dulles sees as a second level, scholars like Karl Rahner and
Carl Peter argue for including under *jus divinum* institutional features that appeared after the apostolic age but

had a biblical basis and seemed to express the very nature of the church. Such features would include three other sacraments: confirmation, marriage, and the anointing of the sick. Perhaps they would also include the papal and episcopal ministries.

One would be hard put to define the line between these levels exactly, but they yet are distinguishable from Dulles' third level. Here lodge temporary, reversible developments that yet seem to have derived from Christ's will and the Spirit's inspiration. A positive and contemporary example might be the sense that God wills a less juridical and more consensus-oriented form of ecclesiastical leadership, i.e., a greater collegiality. A negative example might be the cardinalate, patriarchate, and archiepiscopacy—hierarchical grades that were never clearly mandated. Dulles finds these beset with ecumenical issues, since the separated churches tend to ask one another for the continuance of the structures they have evolved historically. Catholics, for example, ask for the maintenance of a papal form for the Petrine ministry. Women, for a Catholic counterexample, ask that their historic exclusion from orders be reversed. On this point, Dulles' judicious openness seems a bit timid:

A more difficult question, still under debate, is that of the ordination of women. As with the papacy, so here, it would not be enough to argue simply from apostolic precedent or from unbroken continuity in the past. If the exclusion of women from ordination is to be sustained, a justification must be given in terms of the biblical and liturgical symbolism and the needs of the Church as a sign of Christ in the world today. The Congregation for the Doctrine of the Faith, in its Declaration of October 15, 1976, held that the reservation of priestly ordination to men corresponds to "God's plan for the Church," but the rationale for this decision continues to be debated. It is important for the universal Church not to let itself become bound, even unconsciously, to the sociocultural conditions of a dying age.[14]

The fourth and final level concerns discretionary matters, what Lutheranism called "adiaphora," or matters of indifference, and scholasticism called "law merely ecclesiastical." Here it would not be helpful to speak of divine law, except perhaps in a permissive sense.

Overall, recent ecumenical discussion has injected considerable nuance into the notion of the church's divine right. Bilateral studies of such thorny issues as the Petrine ministry, Mary, and infallibility have brought Catholics and Protestants to considerable agreement. Because Protestant ecclesiological evolution varies among the different Protestant churches, it is easier to characterize Roman Catholic evolution. For instance, in the influential work of Karl Rahner, both prior to Vatican II and subsequently, one can see a growing attention to history and personal freedom, with a corresponding criticism of static authoritarianism. The work of other Roman Catholic ecclesiologists derives explicitly from Protestant biblicism.

The Orthodox position on these issues is complex and far from monolithic. In general, however, Orthodox ecclesiology has lately taken a more active ecumenical turn, as Michael Fahey's recent survey shows in detail.[15] In preparation for a forthcoming Pan-Orthodox Great and Holy Council, and for the first international official dialogue between Pan-Orthodoxy and the Roman Catholic Church, a flurry of theological consultations among the various Orthodox bodies is afoot, as well as consultations between Orthodox and Roman Catholics, Anglicans, Protestants, and Jews.

Within Orthodoxy itself the central ecclesiological

agenda include the situation of Orthodox living in the "diaspora," i.e., in countries not traditionally Orthodox; "autocephaly," the canonical independence of certain churches; promotion of the autonomy of churches; the order of commemorations in the Divine Liturgy; calendar reform; marriage impediments; fasting regulations; ecumenism; and social justice. These largely pastoral topics reflect both the problems that the Orthodox churches share among themselves and the practical issues that divide them from other Christians.

Concerning the official dialogue with Roman Catholics, it appears that the main focus of discussion will be the common vision of the sacramental life that both churches share. Papal primacy is still a serious problem, but another may be Orthodox theology's relative unconcern with modern historical-critical biblical scholarship and its cautious reaction to secularization. These also affect Orthodoxy's dialogue with Protestants, as does its fierce stand against the ordination of women, which latter caused Orthodoxy to criticize sharply the 1976 decision of the Episcopal Church U.S.A. to admit women to the priesthood.

There may be still deeper differences between the basic vision of Eastern Orthodoxy and that of the West. Alexander Schmemann has called these "the main cause of that 'failure' which characterizes the ecumenical encounter between Orthodoxy and the West—a failure which cannot be concealed by the massive presence of Orthodox officials at all ecumenical gatherings, and which is not less real and profound even if the majority of Orthodox are unaware of it."[16]

Ecclesiology, then, has recently been agitated by a number of ecumenical issues that have pressured all theologians to reflect more deeply on both the essential nature of the church and its political articulation of this nature—

"church order." Dulles' sacramental metaphor for the
church represents the tendency of many theologians to
conceive the church as the social body that formally represents Christ to the world. In the context of a case-study
approach to the articles of the Christian creed, Robert A.
Evans has stressed the image of the church as a community in the hope that this may move church members away
from the overemphasis on "domain and task" which spotlights structures to the neglect of the action of the Holy
Spirit. Evans' preference for community stems especially
from Protestant ecclesiological experience, and perhaps
radical Reformed churches would applaud it as superior to
Dulles on the Spirit. That is, perhaps they would feel that
it does better justice to the power that makes of the
church a "sacrament."

In Evans' own terms: "The distinctive element in the
life of the Church is the experience of the Holy Spirit in
our midst which creates a new quality of human relatedness known as *communitas*." *Communitas* he translates in
terms of encounters of intimate support among persons
who so love and care for one another that they celebrate
a gift of abundant life in their midst. Its ecclesiological
implications are significant: "*Communitas* as envisaged
here can never be created—only celebrated. It is not a
possession, but a gift. *Communitas* is not hierarchical, but
rather egalitarian. *Communitas* is not static, but trans-
formative. *Communitas* is the transpersonal embodiment
of Christ's grace."[17] Even as emphases rather than dogmatic theses, this calls for a freer church life than is now
envisioned by the church bodies to the right.

Ministry to Word and Sacrament

If the division of the church has finally made progress
toward ecumenical unity a widely sensed imperative, the

ecclesiology of today's ecumenical atmosphere yet retains many traditional themes. One of these themes, sacramentality, we saw to be central in Avery Dulles' Roman Catholic reflections on divine church law. *Communitas,* we may assume, also entails sacramental expressions for the interactions that embody Christ's grace, since it is a conception flowing from the Reformed sense of the church as "the congregation of saints wherein the Gospel is rightly preached and the sacraments rightly administered."[18] Still, there seems little doubt that preaching and Scripture could function more prominently in many a Protestant ecclesiology than they now do, insisting that it is God's Word that forms the church, God's Word that renders congregations really the body of Christ. In the ecumenical ecclesiology now struggling to be born, Word and Sacrament will have to indwell in one another, like Son and Spirit.

An excellent treatment of this theme is Bernard Cooke's *Ministry to Word and Sacraments.* [19] In it he investigates the history and theology of the church's diaconal structure, its commission to service. From New Testament times, offices in the church have been intended to serve the people of God and the world. The ministerial power that God entrusted to the church has been evident in its evolution at five specific points: forming community, proclaiming God's word, caring for the needs of God's people (physical and spiritual alike), carrying out God's judgment, and instituting sacramental life.

The first function, forming community, is related to Evans' notion of *communitas,* as also to what is of divine constitution in the church. As Cooke's conclusion reads: "If there is one basic conclusion that can be drawn from this first part of our study, it is that decisions about the retention, change, abolition, or inception of ministries in the Church must be governed by the evolving needs and opportunities of the Church."[20] This does not abolish the notion that church offices can be of divine origin, but it does set them in a dynamic, charismatic context, where God, or Christ as originator, stays very active in church history.

The other ministries also take shape in this dynamic context. Concerning ministry to God's word, for instance, Cooke begins his theological reflection with the assurance that "there has always been in all the various Christian traditions an acknowledgement that a certain primacy attaches to the preaching and explanation of the word of God." He concludes, however, that the various services into which the ministry to God's word divides all "flow from the basic prophetic and sacramental nature of the Christian community itself, that is, from the indwelling presence of the incarnated Word and of the Spirit. It is the people of God that is the revelation, the word of God; the various ministries we have described are organs by which this believing community nurtures and expresses its prophetic existence. Whatever need there is for a particular ministry of the word is rooted in a basic need of the community as word. This is the principle that must guide us today in our practical examination of the ministry of the word."[21]

Cooke's treatments of service, judgment, and sacramentality are similarly functionally oriented. They, as many other recent ecclesiological investigations, show that what we are finally talking about in a theology of the church is revelation and the incarnation. How does the Christian God continue to be present in the world? There is no people of *God,* no word of *God,* no sacrament as an act of

Christ, unless the gracious love that is God as spirit creates material signs which convey to humankind something of divine life. The greatest material sign is the incarnation of the Logos, Jesus. The records of Israel precede it and memoried interpretations follow it. From it flow the rites of initiation, communion, and forgiveness which act out Christian faith.

Perhaps liturgists recognize this best. Though the present membership of the North American Academy of Liturgy is only about two hundred and fifty, the theology it reflects is sacramental, biblical, and ecumenical in ecclesiologically distinctive ways. Indeed, liturgists seem to be moving beyond their previous concern for rubrics and ceremonial, toward a more synthetic grasp of what ought to happen in Christian worship. Thus, James F. White can approach what he calls five basic types of Christian worship, the non-eucharistic Sunday morning service, the Lord's Supper, Christian initiation, weddings, and funerals, with an Augustinian paraphrase: "Know what you are doing and do as you please."

What this means is to remember or refocus the good news, the grace of salvation incarnate in Jesus, on a particular occasion in order to help actualize the church. To do this well today, when enthusiastic experimentation has somewhat run its course, calls for the following: inclusiveness, so that all types of church members are considered; imagination, so that the good news stays new; attention to the humanity, the corporeality, of the people the news addresses; ecumenical desire both to draw from the full Christian treasury and to serve church unity; and social responsibility, so that the poor hear a news *they* can call good.[22]

LIBERATION AND HUMAN RIGHTS

The central social issue is justice. Since the age when Plato, Zoroaster, the Hebrew prophets, Confucius, and other visionaries clarified the meaning of conscience, justice has fascinated humankind. Recent political theology in Europe and Latin America has taken the biblical imperatives for justice into the heart of theological reflection. Thus, Juan Luis Segundo has spoken of the liberation of theology, José Miranda has conjoined Marx and the Bible, Dorothee Soelle has recast the Protestant interpretation of sin in political terms. In their work, the conflict between a religious vision of justice and present injustices forces theology to conceive Jesus as a *liberator*. Socially speaking, what must Jesus do? He must liberate us from disease, poverty, and the despair that results from the greed of the powerful. At the level of vision and heart, Jesus offers a new way, a new power of health and hope.[23]

On the American scene, a significant coalition of theologians is at work trying to translate these intuitions into a program that fits our peculiar situation. *Theology in the Americas*[24] is a collection of papers given at the Detroit Conference of August 1975, in which Latin Americans, blacks, women, American Hispanics, and other American minorities participated. Since Detroit these groups seem to be more sympathetic to one another than they had been. For instance, statements from the National Conference of the Black Theology Project held in Atlanta in August 1977 are less antipathetic to women's liberation.

One of the most lucid responses from the main-line churches to liberation theology is that of Robert McAfee Brown, who begins *Theology in a New Key* with a brief history of Roman Catholic, Protestant, and Orthodox theologies of social justice, and of the genesis of Latin-

American liberation thought, starting with the Latin-American Bishops Conference of 1968 at Medellín.[25] Key developments there included assuming the viewpoint of the poor, appreciating how the deepest poverty actually affects the Latin-American majority, and admitting the existence of class conflict.

Latin-American theologians found that such points can be developed into a hermeneutic of hope, reading Scripture for the fresh initiatives God offers there, a scenario quite opposed to those which have dominated both traditional Latin-American Catholicism and capitalist American Christianity. In the biblical scenario, God sides with the poor and blesses the oppressed.

Brown concludes that the church does indeed defend the poor. The Pastoral Letter by the Roman Catholic bishops of Appalachia on powerlessness, for instance, he finds incisive. Christian liturgy is also a resource of great potential, for there it is impossible to avoid the biblical God. Christian internationalism supplies a horizon and a communications network which could be crucially helpful to the global poor. But the question remains whether the affluent, many of whom are nominal Christians, will find the faith to begin the renunciation and redistribution which justice demands. Brown is hopeful, but not optimistic.

Frederick Lawrence has examined the foundations of political theology from the very different perspective of the Lonergan school and has come to a parallel conclusion.[26] Behind it is a highly sophisticated cognitional theory lately in dialogue with German political thought, especially that of the Frankfurt "critical school" and with Marx's challenge to move society toward social justice. Throughout their debate over ideology, consciousness, and technical versus practical reason, Continental think-

ers have grappled with those disorders of human awareness which cause Western society's difficulties.

The Lonerganian response accepts this problematic, but
does not accept the Continental neo-Kantian and neo-
Marxist solutions. First, from the standpoint of classical
philosophy, these neglect those aspects of human reason
which are neither technical nor practical. Second, from
the standpoint of Christian faith, they neglect the moral
impotence of human sinfulness. In its depths, reason has
a pure desire to know things as they are that is neither
technical nor practical. This pure desire is finally directed
to God, who alone grounds the world. However, the vigorous exercise of such reason is so rare that "realists" from
Machiavelli to Locke discount it. For them, human beings
are irrational, without a contemplative core, and thus they
design political arrangements to function irrationally. Unless conversion occurs, their counsels of despair find little
opposition.

With conversion, though, a horizon of unrestricted love
can stabilize contemplative reason and link it to resolute
praxis. Then the God we intend as ground and term is
graciously present and personally self-giving. A firm balance, including a firm sense of justice, may then emerge.
Of course, the disorder of society is such that those whom
grace stabilizes in reason are likely to be few. Through
deculturation, societies tend by degrees toward cycles of
decline in which rationality and love seem utopian.

In such periods, faith that would do justice must realize
that redemption follows the law of the cross. Only suffering love is powerful, dramatic, and unearthly enough to
dent deculturation. Only *doing* the gospel shows the way
to liberation. Lawrence joins Robert McAfee Brown in the
claim that the liberating theology of justice goes theoreti-
cally and practically alike to the law of the cross.

Human Rights

While prophetic vigor and biblical speech are proper to the work of the liberation theologians, a more analytic discussion of ethical principles and human rights is more generally the case in the United States today. In *Protestant and Roman Catholic Ethics,* James M. Gustafson has tried to locate the consensus which Protestant and Roman Catholic ethics have recently achieved. For example, where traditional Catholic ethics stressed being, nature, and law, it recently emphasizes becoming, history, and grace. Conversely, Protestant ethics, whose predilection was for the dynamic side, has lately more place for structure, order, and stability. Since such a dialectical combination of opposites is presently not in favor, the next stage of the ecumenical harmonization of ethics may go rather slowly. Gustafson is quite sensitive to this: "It also means that many persons in the churches of both traditions will disparage the requisite work as 'academic,' 'nit-picking,' 'tedious,' and unrelated to the burning issues of the day."[27]

Gustafson's desire to get to the basic principles of coherent ethical theory reflects a healthy interest in the contemplative reason. Thus, one may well read his final thesis on the state of ecumenical ethics in a quite positive sense: *"Any more fundamental convergence will occur only when there is more consensus on the basic outlook, principle, or metaphor that is appropriate to Christian theological ethics* that will provide the center of a comprehensive, coherent view."[28] Insofar as the achieving of this consensus demands analytic description, Gustafson would refocus ethics in theology proper.

The final work we will discuss in this chapter draws together the major themes we have dealt with. David Hollenbach's *Claims in Conflict*[29] is historical insofar as it tries to recapitulate the Catholic human rights tradition of the past one hundred years. It is cultural insofar as that tradition, represented especially by papal encyclicals since Leo XIII, constituted an evolving commentary on modern Western culture. Hollenbach shows one portion of the Christian church ministering the word, and he is well aware of the international economics which so concern liberation theology.

Claims in Conflict begins by arguing that human rights are presently in a theoretical vacuum. On one side, the liberal democratic tradition dominant in the United States so values individual political freedoms that it is slow to confront mass economic, social, and cultural injustices. On the other side, Soviet Marxism so concentrates on these latter factors that it overlooks individual political rights. These have consistently clashed in the United Nations, but without the results one might hope for. Present analysts realize that these are merely different modes of implementation, but precisely how to conceive the social humanity that is their object remains uncertain.

Hollenbach hopes that nongovernmental agencies, such as the Roman Catholic Church, might illumine this problem. Toward this end, he traces the development of Roman Catholic rights theory. From Leo XIII's encyclical *Rerum Novarum* of 1891 to the statements of the Synod of Bishops in 1971, its principal theme has been the dignity of the human person. For Leo XIII, this issue was economic: human dignity entails rights to food, clothing, shelter, and adequate wages. For Pius XI (1922–1939), the injustices of the social and economic *institutions* which provide material goods were most important. Pius XII (1939–1958) emphasized public morality. *Pacem in Terris* (1963) of John XXIII (1958–1963) systematically related the dignity of the human person to the new, internationally interdependent, economic order. In the Vatican II

declaration *Gaudium et Spes* (1965), Catholic awareness
of international complexity took on an evolving, commu-
nal character. Thus Paul VI's *Populorum Progressio* (1967)
and *Octogesima Adveniens* (1971) dealt with the historicity of social institutions. Like *Justice in the World*, the
statement of the 1971 Synod of Bishops, these defined
justice as granting all peoples the right to development.
The primary criterion they offered for discerning human
indignity, it followed, was lack of participation in the processes of development.

Though there remain problems in gathering these developments into a fully coherent vision that is realistic
about social conflict, recent discussion has attempted this
through the specifically Christian norm of love: "All the
doctrines and symbols of the Christian faith—creation of
all persons by the one God, the universal graciousness of
God toward all, the redemption of all by Christ, and the
call of all persons to share in the mystery of Christ's death
and resurrection—all these are the foundation of a conception of mutual love and human solidarity that is richer
than any philosophical or empirical discussion of the mutual obligations of human beings toward each other,
whether liberal or Marxist."[30]

Practically, the norm of love means that when conflicts
arise between the claims of the poor and the claims of the
rich, the claims of the poor should receive priority. Quite
strictly, persons in need have a *right* to necessities, which
precedes the rights of others to luxuries. Thus, the fundamental dignity of the human person and the destiny of the
earth's goods for *all* the earth's people begin to pressure
public policy.

Hollenbach's concluding chapter, "Towards Policy,"
argues that the norm of love, as well as a sophisticated
awareness of complexity in current social life, renders

inadequate the common tendency to present rights decisions as trade-offs between economic well-being and political liberty. Rather, we must rise to a position where we
can see human rights policy in terms of the *interconnec-
tions* between the different aspects of human dignity that
demand respect. Brazil illustrates this principle dramati-
cally, albeit by default. The Brazilian military regime has
severely restricted civil liberties such as freedom of the
press and the right of unions to organize. It has also employed torture, imprisonment, and assassination. The result has been the extreme political marginalization of all
dissenters. Further, while the top 5 percent of Brazilian
income earners increased their share of the national income from 27.4 to 36.3 percent between 1960 and 1970,
the bottom 80 percent saw their share decrease from 45.5
percent to 36.8 percent in the same period. Thus, the
Brazilian poor have grown ever more marginalized
economically.[31]

This is precisely the sort of interconnection a human
rights policy is intended to offset. Such a policy is moved
by the strategic convictions that: "(1) The needs of the
poor take priority over the wants of the rich. (2) The freedom of the dominated takes priority over the liberty of the
powerful. (3) The participation of marginalized groups
takes priority over the preservation of an order which
excludes them."[32] Only the culpably unimaginative will
not see how these apply to the United States. Christians of
the 1980s, it seems, must insist that it is time for profiteers
to beware.

CHAPTER 4

Self

From an overview of theological methods and through studies of recent literature on nature and society, we have come closer to theology's human source. "Theology," after all, is really an abstraction, an abbreviation for what theologians do. The correlations of our discussion pass through the self, the concrete center of awareness. Remembering Freud's dictum that mature selfhood or personality involves the abilities to love and to work, we shall discuss sex, work, and, as a religious supplement to Freud's dyad, prayer. To launch this discussion we must first consider the life cycle, for it is an interest in how human beings develop, especially in their adult years, that has set the tone for recent religious psychology.

THE LIFE CYCLE

Clinician and theoretician Erik Erikson has so humanized and broadened psychoanalytic insights that he has made them clearly relevant to a variety of fields and problems, including religion. Religious concerns are among the virtues around which he structures his life-cycle schemata. His work has included full-length studies of Luther and Gandhi as prototypes of young adulthood and maturity, and he has stimulated many other studies which have employed his ideas.

To epitomize the schemata of the man to whom all four of our major sources in this section refer, we shall draw on Erikson's recent essay, "Dr. Borg's Life-Cycle."[1] Erikson's method in this essay is to analyze the character revelation of the protagonist in Ingmar Bergman's film *Wild Strawberries*. In the course of journeying to Lund to receive an honorary degree that will cap his fifty-year medical career, Isak Borg, aged seventy-six, passes through a series of dreams and encounters which lay bare to Erikson's clinical eye all the major crises of the life cycle. The advantage to this film is that it keeps Erikson's discussion close to life: Isak Borg's life, although only cinematic, is vivid and artistic. A "case" so skillfully drawn by Bergman's intuitive genius, he puts in bold relief the character development we all undergo. By keeping to his predilection for explaining by describing, attentive to concrete details, Erikson reminds us on every page that his theoretical schemata are but tools for clarifying whatever similarities our very disparate life stories may evince when we read them as struggles toward growth.

For Erikson, our personal histories reveal a series of interlocking dialectical conflicts. Together, they produce a dynamic epigenesis, the achievement of maturity from inbuilt drives and demands. For each conflict, and therefore for each life-cycle stage, there is a "virtue," a power or personal capacity, being acquired. The successful resolution of the "crisis" of infancy, for example, is the acquisition of the most basic virtue, hope. Hope is the advantage, slight or great, that an infant comes to have over its mistrust. Mistrust never completely recedes. Indeed, it should not. Life is such that it furnishes us good reasons for mistrust. But psychic health requires some margin of trust over mistrust, enough, at least, to enable us to go on living. Throughout our years, in fact, we need hope and in the most pathological cases, hopelessness is often the existential core. Thus, from his clinical observation Erikson has tried to sketch the ordinary ways people struggle for personal growth through the ordinary clashes of trust and mistrust through which come the virtues such as hope, which they ordinarily must acquire.

Briefly, then, Erikson's list of virtues includes hope, will, purpose, competence, fidelity, love, care, and wisdom. In infancy, trust clashes with mistrust and the result is *hope*. In early childhood, autonomy clashes with shame and doubt to produce *will. Purpose* is the virtue that the play age must fashion from the conflicts between initiative and guilt. During the school years, industry battles inferiority for *competence*. "Childhood," then, ought progressively to develop our capacities for dealing with the world in a balanced way, that is, hopefully, willfully, purposefully, and competently. Each of these virtues builds upon its predecessor and none of them (and none of their constituent conflicts) is ever discarded. Throughout life we keep trying to develop a richer and simpler synthesis.

Identity versus diffusion of identity, "identity crisis," is the conflict Erikson is best known for having described. It is the adolescent battleground for the epigenesis of *fidelity*. With fidelity, "the ability to sustain loyalties freely pledged in spite of the inevitable contradictions and confusions of value systems," one can begin to try to meet the demands of young adulthood, where one's desires for intimacy clash with the fears or needs that cause isolation. *Love* is the virtue of young adulthood, a balanced victory of intimacy over isolation. And what is Eriksonian love? It is "mutuality of devotion forever subduing the antagonisms inherent in divided function."[2]

In maturity, love is drawn up into *care,* so long as the clash between generativity and self-absorption comes to a positive resolution. Care is "the widening concern for what has been generated by love, necessity, or accident; it overcomes the ambivalence arising from irreversible obligation." Finally, in old age our genes and psyche ask us to ripen to an integrity, a wholeness, that is stronger than the despair and disgust which may afflict us. As there are good, realistic grounds for identity diffusion, isolation, and self-absorption, so there are good grounds for viewing life in the round and feeling disgust. Evil and negativity are the inevitable foes. *Wisdom,* then, represents the ability to find an integrity greater than these. It is "the detached and yet active concern with life itself in the face of death itself, and . . . it maintains and conveys the integrity of experience, in spite of the decline of bodily and mental functions."[3]

Pastoral Applications

I have discussed Erikson's descriptions of the adult virtues of fidelity, love, care, and wisdom because they are foremost in the pastoral applications one finds in the recent theological literature. A good example of such applications is Donald Capps's recent *Pastoral Care.*[4] Although Capps is indebted to other developmental psychologists, Erikson seems most influential on his "thematic" approach to the religious personality. This approach focuses on the recurring patterns that give a particular person his or her distinctive "character," and it is sensitive to the threads that seem to weave the person's biography, his or her story. In the most explicitly theological of his chapters, Capps tries to correlate a list of theological themes from Paul W. Pruyser's *The Minister as Diag-*

nostician[5] with Erikson's eight epigenetic virtues. The correlation looks like this:

Providence–Hope
Grace–Will
Repentance–Purpose
Vocation–Competence
Faith–Fidelity
Communion–Love
Vocation–Care
Awareness of the Holy–Wisdom

To simplify our discussion, let us restrict ourselves to the four "adult" theological themes of faith, communion, vocation, and awareness of the holy. Faith is the theological quality at issue in the "adolescent" conflict between identity and identity diffusion. To discern and promote faith, the religious counselor can focus on "the counselee's affirmative attitude toward life; his experience of his religious proclivities as widening his scope of engagement."[6] This is a theme whose presence or absence may be telltale. By sensitivity to such motifs, the pastoral counselor can grasp the counselee's problems, the counselee's self. Of course, the counselor is not a mechanic checking out a machine, and no scheme exactly fits the complicated actuality of a given person. But insofar as the set of theological themes is an adequate inventory of the attitudes of a mature religious personality, it brings a measure of clarity to the counselor's work.

Thus, "communion" may clarify whether the counselee feels "accepted into the social groups that matter to him." It represents a successful resolution or mediation of the conflict between intimacy and isolation. Similarly, vocation "focuses on the counselee's sense of purpose, dedication, personal competence, and effectiveness." It represents good results in the dialectical struggle between generativity and stagnation. Finally, "awareness of the holy" focuses on "the counselee's relationship to powers or forces beyond himself." For Capps it is the theological equivalent of wisdom, the resolution of the conflict between integrity and despair.

Capps provides helpful case studies for these theological themes, as for other matters in his book. He also provides a table that further correlates Pruyser's theological themes with the descriptions that Robert Jay Lifton has given of today's "protean" personality, the rather fluid, unstructured self that the historical dislocations of modernity, and its mass of new information, have created.

By the time one has sifted through all this psychological correlation, one theological fact is obvious: pastoral care, as Capps conceives it, has little to do with overtly Christian interpretations of the experiential self, but at the most, with a rather bland, not specifically Christian, "theology": "It can be argued that a theological diagnosis might well provide a fresher *psychological* understanding . . . than many psychological interpretations would afford." However, the protean personality does not resonate very well to theology: "Not only do people fail to experience the positive influence of God in their lives but also they no longer experience the absence of God's positive influence as a personal lack or loss. . . . Theological themes such as providence, faith, grace, and repentance simply lack any relevance at all."[7] Capps provides no reference to Jesus, the Spirit, providence, or grace to counter this. Where a theologian might reinterpret the protean personality, resolute in the conviction that God is greater than our problem, Capps relinquishes God's significance without a whimper.

More explicitly Christian and theological in their appro-

priation of Erikson to pastoral care are Evelyn and James
Whitehead. Their recent *Christian Life Patterns*[8] is an
exposition in religious terms of the adult portions of the
life cycle, replete with sacramental and ecclesial implications. Because they are open to overtly Christian experience and conception, the Whiteheads can tap traditional
Christian wisdom about the self unavailable to Capps.

Drawing upon the work of developmental psychologists
such as Daniel Levinson,[9] who have tried to examine the
adult decades more closely than Erikson has, the Whiteheads offer religious adults a sharp profile to contemplate.
For instance, concerning the issues of mid-life, the early
forties, they suggest the interplay of the three themes of
personal power, care, and interiority. Personal power generally relates to competence at work. Mid-life is a time
when experience, seniority, and developed skills have pre-
pared a person to assume leadership and responsibility.
Unless the talents one has developed find suitable opportunities for use, frustration is likely to follow. Actually, this
is only a specification of the pervading desire of mid-life
persons to generate and to care. Middle-aged adults need
to be needed, by children, younger colleagues, the institutions where they work, and the community at large. Finally, the middle years are also regularly a time when
greater interiority beckons. One has spent enough time in
this profession, this marriage, and this self to want to reflect on its adequacy. For some persons such reflection is
frightening or depressing. For others it opens a new door.

Reconciling oneself to the shortfalls of one's early
dreams; bringing the masculine/feminine, active/passive
polarities of the self into greater balance; becoming a men-
tor who stimulates creativity in others—these are other
ways that the middle years achieve a capacity in one to
widen out, let go of old ambitions, and accept more of life's

ambiguity. In Christian terms, they are years when *dia-konia,* or service, and stewardship contrast themselves to a greater sense of confusion: one has greater responsibilities but also a keener sense that few of the simple verities remain. Still, with strong community support we usually can bear both the burdens and the opportunities of the middle years with grace.

The same is true regarding the burdens and opportunities of old age. Integrity, the positive wholeness that old age struggles to gain, is for Erikson quite religious. Quite naturally, it inclines us to communicate with what he calls "that ultimate other." The Christian subsumption of integrity under biblical faith tends to show itself as a personal testimony to life's spiritual significance. Out of scriptural and liturgical symbols, I affirm that the God of Jesus holds *my* time, gives *my* declining life rich meaning. Perhaps this is the ultimate blessing Christianity bestows on the life cycle. Loving the life of Christ in the face of death, the aging believer receives a wisdom in depth. Christian tradition long has associated such wisdom with the Holy Spirit. More and more, the Spirit uses the personality's completion, and the body's coming to term, to assume command. For the community, the Spirit's effect on the aged is an invaluable resource. As Erikson consistently has shown, the life cycle links generations and is thus socially crucial. Were the church fully to utilize its aged, to utilize their anamnesis, their ability to remember the whole in hope-filled terms, it could create a new and coherent heart in protean secular society.

Life Stories

An interesting event in recent theology is the connection of developmental religious psychology to the theology of literature through "story." Autobiography, psychohistory, and "history" itself all lend themselves to literary analogy as narratives. "God made man because he loves stories," concludes the Hasidic tale at the head of Elie Wiesel's *The Gates of the Forest*. [10] The "he" in the sentence is ambiguous, deliberately so, one suspects. Both God and we human beings love stories. By the word of God's mouth the heavens were made and by naming a child we start a life script, a biography. Standing for artists everywhere, Ingmar Bergman analyzes current existence through angular, constricted life stories of persons like Dr. Borg. Standing for therapists everywhere, Erik Erikson probes the dynamics by which the psyche speaks or misspeaks itself. Theologians, more aware now that Scripture is their own master story, have lately produced richer and more personal appreciations of scriptural metaphor, the fertile imagination through which Scripture communicates its meaning.

John Shea's *Stories of God* is part of this theological trend. Especially interesting for our purposes is its beginning chapter, "Exceeding Darkness and Undeserved Light," because its point of departure is a statement of Erikson's: "Religion . . . elaborates on what feels profoundly true even though it is not demonstrable; it translates into significant words, images, and codes the exceeding darkness which surrounds man's existence, and the light which pervades it beyond all desert or comprehension." [11]

As the quotation suggests, Shea is more resonant to divine mystery than either Capps or the Whiteheads. Although he does not refer to Karl Rahner, he moves the self's story to the horizon of mystery that Rahner has used to refashion theology's understanding of human personality. Rahner's human personality, his religious "self," is a "hearer of the word." It waits for mystery to disclose itself.

Shea's self is a story in the telling whose chapters lead to mystery: "The fact that we have a biography at all reveals another relatedness, a relatedness which suffuses yet transcends these environments. This relationship is more elusive than the others and often goes unacknowledged. But when it bursts into consciousness (and that is how it usually enters), it rivets the psyche and its importance is beyond question. We are inescapably related to Mystery."[12]

We realize this inescapable relation in myriad ways. Sensing our contingency, we may wonder why anything exists at all. That was Leibniz' basic question, raised in our own day by Martin Heidegger. It underscores the mystery of being, of existing, that is, of the fact that any thing stands forth from nothingness. The mother giving birth marvels at the mystery of the body. Somehow, beyond her control, nature has reached through her nerves to her spirit. Still more mysterious invitations come from the dialogue and communion of love. The contemporary self is not so protean that it has lost its core relation. For Kierkegaard, the self was a relation to the Absolute. For Shea, the self is a tale of mysterious potential.

Indeed, mystery is the most basic reality we encounter, wherever we go, before and behind. Therefore, "if Mystery is absurd, then all our proximate meanings are the camouflages of death. If Mystery is not the source of healing, then our partial reconciliations are only momentary traces. Mystery, because of its pervasive and intimate character, either grounds or undermines our deepest hopes and loves. . . . In this situation and with this awareness we do a distinctively human thing. We gather together and tell stories of God to calm our terror and hold our hopes on high."[13]

Shea moves from this biographic account to a theory of the world-making that narration brings about, and then to a fresh look at the Christian story. In the end, this is clearly more theology than religious psychology, and it has shown itself to have the crucial requisites for an adequate theology of the self. Such a theology would illumine the life cycle as a story of covenant. It would describe developmental crises in their full dimensions by sacramentalizing them. In terms of the Christian covenant, God has wed the self. Thus, God shares all the self's years and bestows upon them their meaning. "Mystery" describes God's presence in all the chapters of all selves' stories. It directs divinity's very constitution of human awareness to the dynamics of the life cycle. All meaning derives from mystery, all meaning entails mystery.

SEX

In thinking about themselves, contemporary men and women ponder their sexual identities as their forebears in faith did not. The further reaches of such pondering go to the very core of theology, where the concept of God itself undergoes feminist critique, as well as to marriage, work, church office, politics, historiography, and culture.

The theoretical work currently most exciting to feminists is Dorothy Dinnerstein's *The Mermaid and the Minotaur,* a book that concentrates on child-rearing, seeing it as the key to what it calls "sexual arrangements and the human malaise." Sexual arrangements are "the division of responsibility, opportunity, and privilege that prevails between male and female humans." Human malaise refers to "our species' normal psychopathology, which has pervaded our cultural—and perhaps even the most recent stages of our physical—evolution, the maladaptive stance, chronically uncomfortable and at this point critically life-threatening, that humanity maintains toward itself and

toward nature." The link between these two conceptions
provides Dinnerstein her reason for saying that: "until we
grow strong enough to renounce the pernicious prevailing
forms of collaboration between the sexes, both man and
woman will remain semi-human, monstrous."[14]

The mermaid and the minotaur symbolize our current
inhumanity, our monstrosity. Dinnerstein sees the mermaid as treacherous, the seductive, impenetrable female
who represents the dark, magic water from which life
comes. She lures voyagers to their doom. The minotaur is
fearsome, the gigantic, eternally infantile offspring of unnatural lust. He is male power as mindless, greedy, and
insatiably devouring of human flesh. Out of her background as a social scientist, with special reference to
Freudian and Gestalt psychology, Dinnerstein wants to
clarify why people continue to consent to arrangements
which spawn this malaise. She specifically wants to clarify
how we brought it about that "for virtually every living
person it is a woman—usually the mother—who has provided the main initial contact with humanity and with
nature."[15]

En route to clarifying this, Dinnerstein elaborates the
implications of women's dominance in child-rearing. First,
there is the enormous influence that any dominant adult
would have on a newborn, who is totally vulnerable in its
first experiences. Second, from the fact that women are
these dominant adults come such consequences as a double standard of sexual behavior, women's and men's mutual views of each another as overgrown children, and
many types of antagonism toward women, most of them
shared by women for each other.

The double standard of sexual behavior is Dinnerstein's
central analytic observation. Men have a monopoly on
making history. In their collusion to keep women bound

to child-rearing, men and women have essentially defined the public realm as male. Thus, by and large it is only men who have been free to go to war, to the laboratory, and on the political campaign trail. Further, this aspect of the double standard has as its complement that "since it is he whose sexual impulsivity is legitimate, while she is expected to be receptive and undemanding, it is he, not she, at whose initiative erotic energy can with propriety be withdrawn from love and invested in worldly affairs: She, not he, is the one who must wait when the other turns away and be sexually available when he comes back."[16]

But women's exclusion from making history is far from simple in its consequences. "History-making," in Dinnerstein's lexicon, is shorthand for the outward productivity to which human consciousness is compelled. It is culture, technology, ideas, and material constructs conjoined. Insofar as such "history" represents our humanity specifically, woman's exclusion from it amounts to her demotion to a less than human status. Neither men nor women completely want that. Women resent their marginalization directly enough. On the other hand, they "profit" from it, insofar as they avoid many of history's burdens. The bad faith implicit in such profit prompted Simone de Beauvoir to characterize women's stance as a sort of socially sanctioned existential cowardice. Dinnerstein deepens De Beauvoir's characterization: "The immunity life offers women is immunity not only from the risks and exertions of history-making, but also from the history-maker's legitimate internal misgivings about the value of what he spends his life doing. The use that both sexes make of this female immunity, their mutual motive in fostering it, is in my view the morbid core of our sexual arrangement. To uncover it is the main point of this book."[17]

Dinnerstein makes a similar addition to the motive that

Margaret Mead proposed for women being excluded from history. Mead's thesis, simplified, was that men need cultural creativity to maintain their self-respect in the face of women's biological creativity. Dinnerstein goes beyond this in arguing that both men and women have hoped for peoples outside the history zone who could express their intuition that there is something trivial, empty, ugly, and sad in it. This, however, is deeply neurotic. For men, it leads to the lethal history-making that Lewis Mumford has attributed to the "mega-machine": technology antagonistic to life. Further, it blurs the male vision of the female, until she is both an unworthy outsider and a purer, wiser judge of his male doings. Ultimately men tend to ask their "mother's" blessing on the history they create, and their "mother" both relieves them from history's meaninglessness and punctures their pretensions that history, their great work, is momentous. Thus, men and women cling together and support woman's role as an outsider. Together, they make her both a refuge and a shrewd disillusioner.

The power of Dinnerstein's analysis, the sophistication of which this brief exposition only hints, is its blow at the instinctual roots of our malaise. There, in evolutionary biology and earliest human experience, lie raging emotions which much adult thinking never touches. As we grow to face the fact of our mortality, these emotions figure strongly in the approach-avoidance behavior which mortality generates. Wittingly and unwittingly, men and women have conspired to write a scenario in which men's assumption of history's burdens and privileges and women's perception of history's destructiveness have never been properly matched. Today the ecological implications of this split are massive. The apocalyptic tone of Dinnerstein's argument bespeaks both an awareness of current events such as the nuclear arms race, chemical pollution, and explosive global inequities, and a fierce desire for life. Gloomy though she is about the possibilities, Dinnerstein yet emerges as a champion of life. She is furious about our current arrangements because they show a primal stupidity, perhaps even primal sin. We stand today before two ways, to death and to life. Every time we choose not to know, not to change, not to risk our current comforts, we choose death.

It is the absence of this sort of feminist profundity and passion to affirm life that renders most Christian discussion of sex somewhat colorless. While such an accusation cuts across ecumenical boundaries, Roman Catholic treatments of sex are especially objectionable. After Dinnerstein, surveys such as Francis X. Murphy's "Christianity, Marriage and Sex," James Gustafson's "Theology Confronts Technology and the Life Sciences,"[18] and Richard McCormick's "Notes on Moral Theology: 1978"[19] strike the reader as culpably innocent. Their discussion of sex, love, and life virtually ignore women. If Peter Hebblethwaite's recent report on the Roman Curia's current refusal to laicize Catholic priests is accurate, behind that church's policies lies a deeply neurotic fixation: "The Holy Office experts can conceive of priestly 'failure' only in sexual terms; symptoms of arrogance, pride, domination, authoritarianism, alcoholism can apparently be coped with."[20] One does not have to be especially imaginative or ill-willed to read into this attitude, or into Pope John Paul II's stony response to American nuns who asked him for women's ordination, the ambivalence toward women that Dinnerstein describes.

On the way to postmodern love, then, men and women will have to reform many of their current arrangements. Dinnerstein's book does not assume a horizon of faith, does not speak of a Holy Spirit, of a law of the cross, or of an agape stronger than death. To free these divine energies requires a cultural revolution. There is no isolation of the self from such social factors. The sexual self is a prime candidate for social liberation.

Beyond the social formation of the self, though, remains its inalienable privacy. We still are more than component parts; we still have individual consciences and can pray. Indeed, in the face of the ills of our current social arrangements, contemplative prayer (which we take up below) becomes a political resource. Directly opening the self to God's healing can have enough of the effect of psychotherapy to make men and women lovers more than foes.

WORK

The point of departure in Rosemary Radford Ruether's essay "Home and Work"[21] is the double bind of today's working woman, who usually must run a home in addition to her job. The current split between home and work, far from being traditional, is a fairly recent product of industrialization. In most tribal communities women have been the mainstay of agriculture and handicrafts, because their labors focus in the home and the extended family. Proverbs 31:10–31, the classical text in praise of the virtuous woman, shows Israelite women as productive workers. A similar situation obtained in European peasant society and even in the plantations of the American South. The transition to urban society, however, brought the full exclusion of women from political and professional life, largely because the male cultural arbiters of urban society believed in female inferiority. The result was that women's roles in medicine, handicrafts, and the like shrank markedly.

By the time of industrialization, women were not only

legally dependent on men, as they had been in the patriarchal system, but economically dependent as well. Working
women became "lower class," since "ladies" of leisure and
refinement showed the world what their wealthy and
powerful husbands could afford. Concomitantly, the home
narrowed to a refuge from the ugliness of the "real" world
of male industrial work. Insofar as religion followed this
trend, it became a "feminine" preserve, set equally apart
from the male world of work. Thus women were deemed
too pure to engage in business or politics, as religion was
deemed too pure to be mingled with practical affairs. That
the idealization of women in Victorian times made them
asexual and prompted a whole underworld of prostitution
and pornography suggests that by then this arrangement
had become schizophrenic.

The socialist response to the alienation of labor included
women's emancipation as a major point. Marx and Engels
were explicit on the need to restore women to the world
of production. Thus restored, women would have economic independence and would be free from sexual in-
denture. However, socialist practice in Russia and China
has tended to collectivize work and shrink the family.
"The shrinking of the home, then, becomes the means of
creating the totalitarian society where the self has lost its
autonomous base. Socialists, as well as feminists, must rethink the social role of the home, if they are committed to
a society of freedom as well as a society of equal work
roles." Only in this way can we realistically hope for society possessed of the virtues that the female domestic
sphere traditionally contributed: "co-operation, mutual
support, leisure, celebration, free creativity, and explora-
tion of feelings and personal relations."[22]

In a chapter on Marx's concept of human nature, John
McMurtry argues that creative work is central to the Marx-

ist world view. Indeed, for Marx, human beings begin to raise themselves above the level of animals only when they begin to produce their own means of subsistence. Further, uniquely human work depends on imagination, or "projective consciousness."[23] In this sense, *Homo sapiens* is *Homo faber,* and humanity is thus the band of workers.

Of the different sorts of work that embody this projective consciousness, Marx grants creative art a certain primacy. The "composition" of the writer, for instance, shows human invention and implementation in a pure form, while by contrast most other labor is dominated by outside social forces. Hence, only "posthistorical" Communist society can provide the technical and economic conditions whereby all human labor can approach the status of creative art. Collaboratively or individually, work in the Marxist ideal society should be not alienating but fulfilling.

Probably because of his own historical situation, Marx's illustrations of projective consciousness were more technological in form than his views on creative art might incline one to think. He says, for instance, that "nature builds no machines, no locomotives, railways, electric telegraphs, self-acting mules, etc. . . . These are organs of the human brain, created by the human hand; the power of knowledge, objectified."[24] Nonetheless, this example does not simply capitulate to *Homo technicus.* Marx stressed the conscious planning of social production, and he was indignant at the reduction of human work to mindless specialization. He also blasted the blindness that the profit imperative of capitalism produced, and he disdained projective consciousness that did not move beyond ideas to creative action. The greatest evil of modern technology, in his view, was its destruction of creative intelligence, for human beings have a profound need to realize themselves in the material world through creative work. Indeed, such work is "life's prime want."[25] Thus, however much Marx's socialist successors have destroyed creative work through terrorism and bureaucracy, for this father of socialism it was intrinsic to human health.

If recent reports about work in current American society are accurate, what is intrinsic to human health has for many gone by the boards. Women as a working class suffer special injustices and humiliations, as Louise Kapp Howe's *Pink Collar Workers*[26] more than shows. Studs Terkel begins his oral history of what work means to average Americans with the distressing paragraph: "This book, being about work, is, by its very nature, about violence—to the spirit as well as to the body. It is about ulcers as well as accidents, about shouting matches as well as fistfights, about nervous breakdowns as well as kicking the dog around. It is, above all (or beneath all), about daily humiliations. To survive the day is triumph enough for the walking wounded among the great many of us."[27]

The walking wounded predominate in Terkel's assortment of workers. The spot welder feels that he is only a machine. The bank teller groans that he is caged. The receptionist feels a monkey could replace her. Again and again, "typical" workers feel they are manipulated, treated as objects, as cogs in an inhuman machine. Either they work in clanging factories as adjuncts of gears and pulleys, or they work in uncaring bureaucracies, serving a faceless "system." To be sure, there are exceptions. Terkel met a stonemason in Indiana who took satisfaction in building something excellent. In Chicago he found a piano tuner happy to make possible good music, and in Brooklyn a fireman who fled a bank job for work that makes him feel he does something that counts. And, even for those depressed with their jobs, there are ways to resist boredom and humiliation. There is, for instance, a waitress who tries to lay each plate soundlessly, in order to make service a thing of grace. But the majority of "common laborers" seem shackled to work that underemploys them, in which they find neither challenge nor outlet for their "projective consciousness." As one of Terkel's subjects puts it, "I think most of us are looking for a calling, not a job. Most of us, like the assembly line worker, have jobs that are too small for our spirit. Jobs are not big enough for people."[28]

Creative Work

Responding to this testimony in the context of international economy and ecological crisis, E. F. Schumacher's posthumous *Good Work* begins with a sketch of how we might educate people to good work. Schumacher attacks the notion of the gross national product. First, there is the instructive anomaly that the United States, with its enormous GNP, has degrees of poverty that countries at a much lower GNP do not experience. Second, there is the more intrinsic anomaly that GNP really means nothing qualitative; it is, rather, a purely quantitative measure. Schumacher comments that "statistics don't have to be accurate; they have to be significant. My theory has always been that figures don't mean anything if you can't make them sing. How can anybody assert that 'growth' is a good thing? If my children grow, this is a very good thing; if I should suddenly start growing, it would be a disaster."[29] GNP as a concept bypasses the real question of how we can enhance the quality of life.

Schumacher observes that in the global enonomy there are many extremely poor people and many extremely rich people, but few in the middle. The qualitative implication of this for the extremely rich he puts in Christian terms: "Their job is really to save their souls and they are using far more of the material means than is necessary for this purpose, and it's most likely that therefore they are greatly hindered."[30] By way of a solution, he proposes the distinction between ephemeral goods and eternal goods, between perishable necessities and the deepest expressions of cultural aspirations. Nothing can be more important than the production of an eternal good like a cathedral, but for ephemeral goods the rule should be one of frugality.

Much of Schumacher's considerable imagination and energy has gone into designing a new "intermediate" technology that would help poor countries supply themselves with life's necessities. In no way, then, does he translate "culture of poverty" into destitution. Yet he insists that Western materialism is *not* the good life, and that cultures of poverty often have been qualitatively richer than our Western one. It is ecologically impossible for the world to support consumption at the present Western levels and it is spiritually undesirable. Discovering a better way sets squarely before us the problems of what work ought really to be about.

How can people regain control over their labor, which, after all, takes up the greatest part of their time? Were we to treat them as people in their own right and not just means to an end, and couple this with the distinction between ephemeral and eternal goods elaborated above, we could make a massive advance toward the true good life. Here again Schumacher's philosophy is explicitly religious: "The world has to attach itself to the things that really matter, and not to those ephemeral trivialities which make the most noise. That is the message of religion. I know it is normally handed down in all sorts of other ways, but unless you do that you are an unhappy, messed up person."[31] This relates to the current tragedy of the destruction of the common goods, such as the ecosphere, that are humankind's patrimony. When we lost sight of such simple "religion," we also lost a sense of proportion, restraint, and stewardship. Indeed, we now appear to be completely out of touch with humanity's two great teachers, living nature and traditional, millennial wisdom. No wonder our technological culture seems to be a great machine no one is running.

Were we to put our imaginations to making work fulfilling—to having it engage people's creative faculties, proceed in circumstances limited enough to foster personal interactions, and focus on producing things that met real social needs—we might make economics the spearhead of a return to sanity. Presently, it is the foremost of our oppressors. In good measure, economics now is a problem of scale. Corporations too large to treat people humanly, personally, become inefficient in the most basic terms. Schumacher realizes that at this point his explanation has reached elementary terms: "If the size of the unit is wrong, this means inevitably the eradication to a large extent of T.L.C. Now T.L.C. is the only fertilizer that works. Don't inquire where you can buy it—you can make it yourself. T.L.C. means tender loving care, and this is what our life needs."[32] If we try to organize systems without this, they become unproductive and irrationally expensive. The withdrawal of human labor from agriculture, for instance, has foreclosed agriculture's future, because it is now based on nonrenewable fossil fuels. Instead of working with nature, we bully it. Unfortunately, agriculture is but one of a host of inhumane enterprises.

Briefly, good work goes hand in hand with social sanity and ecological balance. What nourishes the human self, properly conceived, is harmonious with the rest of creation. "Creative" work is not only a fulfilling creation, a *poiēsis,* but it is also an interacting with one's fellow human beings and nature that nurtures the potential of both. This interaction can be discouraging, since it extends from factories to polluted oceans and prisons, but it can also be encouraging. Each opposition to destruction or desacralization extends therapeutically to the other spheres. At the still point of the turning world, both health and disease show a unity. When we start to work well, we will start to love well.

PRAYER

Stipulating that prayer is the principal focus of the Christian religion, contemplatives have sought to root the self in it. In their version, affective love comes to predominate. The result is a certain distancing of Christian contemplation from both Western and non-Christian "meditation." Western meditation, as represented especially by the *Spiritual Exercises* of Ignatius Loyola, became in modern times a discursive, intellectual affair, undertaken to clarify the mind and strengthen the will. Eastern meditation in Hindu or Buddhist forms strove to undercut discursive thinking and reach what Mircea Eliade calls *enstasis,* autonomy or self-possession. Such self-possession does not welcome any emotional attachments or desires. And it does not usually reach out to a personal God, though there are exceptions to this rule. The emphasis of Christian contemplatives on love, then, is distinctive. Even when that love purifies emotional attachments, in dark nights and clouds of unknowing, it yet sanctions a final ardor, a unifying living flame of love.

An intriguing recent work in the tradition of the Russian and Greek Orthodox monastic masters is Sergius Bolshakoff and M. Basil Pennington's *In Search of True Wisdom.* [33] Bolshakoff's contribution is reminiscences of personal encounters he had with great Russian *startsi,* or "spiritual fathers," from before the 1917 revolution. Pennington, a Western Cistercian monk, reports on a number of contacts he made with Greek Orthodox monks in an ecumenical effort to share the fruits of their respective traditions. At the monastery of Meteora in Greece, for instance, he experienced both the charity and the rigidity of Orthodox monasticism. The Monastery of the Transfiguration at Meteora perches atop a rock formation so steep that most supplies have to be hauled up in nets. There a small community of young monks live a life of liturgical and solitary prayer in great simplicity. The abbot, Archimandrite Aimilianos, received Pennington, and while they discussed monasticism quite fraternally, Aimilianos' opening statement, though not in the least offensive, was to the effect that Eastern Orthodoxy has nothing to learn from the West. He also upheld the Orthodox ban on intercommunion, so that Pennington could not participate actively in the eucharistic liturgy. Despite these limitations, they reached some agreement that the life of contemplative prayer is alive and well in both traditions.

On the occasion of the profession of two young monks, Aimilianos preached a conference that expressed the ardor of Orthodox contemplation. It began as follows: "Today, my dear children, we are dancing with joy around the holy altar. Today, again, the Holy Mount is celebrating. Who is so blind as not to see that at this hour heaven is brightly adorned, earth is rejoicing, the martyrs are leaping like surging waves, the saints are singing *Alleluia* to give vent to their desires and sentiments to God as you celebrate your mystical marriage."[34]

The nuptial imagery, which continued through the conference, and the lyric emotionalism are reminiscent of no Western author more than Bernard of Clairvaux, abbot of perhaps the most famous Cistercian monastery. Whatever their legal separation, then, Greeks and Cistercians share a common mystical desire. The various techniques which their traditions employ aim to foster total concentration on God. So too does the famous Eastern "Jesus prayer," which involves constant repetition of the phrase, "Lord Jesus Christ, have mercy on me."

Quite compatible with this Orthodox tradition is the recent Western contemplative interest in a simple prayer of affective love. Much of it is concerned with *The Cloud of Unknowing,* an anonymous fourteenth-century English classic. While Pennington himself has worked to popularize its teaching,[35] the Jesuit William Johnston has edited a modern version of the *Cloud,* compared it with Zen Buddhist experiences (Johnston teaches at Sophia University in Tokyo), and developed from it a full analysis of what a contemporary Christian mysticism entails. Most essentially this is a journey of love: "Throughout this book I have stressed the fact that mysticism is a journey of love. It is the answer to a call of love; and every stage is enlightened and guided by a living flame, a blind stirring, a love which has no reservations or restrictions. This is the love which, Paul says, is superior to any charismatic gift and has no limitations whatsoever."[36]

Readers familiar with classical Western Christian mysticism will notice that Johnston's sentences conflate imagery from John of the Cross ("living flame") and the *Cloud* ("blind stirring"). What these two classical sources share is a conviction that God so exceeds the capacity of the human senses and mind that the best way to union is a comprehensive love from the core of the person, the Bible's "heart," the mystic's "fine point of the spirit." The *Cloud* would have those who find it attractive move from their blind stirring toward wordless, unthinking communion. Indeed, the "cloud" in which such prayer proceeds is precisely the darkening of the senses and intellect. Both easily distract us from the spiritual presence of God. Therefore, at our innermost core, the Spirit would make a prayer of direct loving.

Often it helps if we focus this loving through a single word that we repeat rhythmically, perhaps coordinating it with our breathing. Whatever the method, the point is to attend on God precisely as God, as the mystery too rich for us to grasp. The author of the *Cloud* urges upon us the conviction that active passivity in this mode is the most valuable thing for us. For those whom God calls, it is a venture in being remade, being purified and fulfilled by divine love itself. Johnston argues that God calls many of us to some variant of this. Many of us, he finds, hunger for a simple, silent, direct, comprehensive love of God. We want a being-with, a pure communion with Mystery. It attracts us when busyness becomes a burden, when words or even affections seem gross and contrived. Then we know there must be a still point of integration, totality, and comprehension. We are drawn to it by unknowing, by a dark night of pure loving.

Morton Kelsey's popular work, *The Other Side of Silence*, does not reject the "negative" tradition that Johnston represents, but it does question that tradition's present practicality. Kelsey's predilection is for a more imaginative method that derives largely from Jungian psychology: "Obviously there are not many people who have imageless experiences of such force, and so mysticism became reserved only for the select few. The idea that inner images, which can appear spontaneously to any one of us, might lead beyond one's personal psyche was never considered."[37] By contrast, his own method tries to tap the force of our psychic images, both waking and dreaming. In ways reminiscent of Loyola's "application of the senses," he would have the mediator picture Christ, speak with him, and converse personally. The point is to *use* the imagination rather than undercut it. Alternatively, the point is to use our psychodynamics, since they have a great say in whether we feel compunction, joy, faith, and the like, that is, whether we actually experience the things of religion as real.

One can see, then, that the postmodern self still hungers for God. Responding to the advances that psychology and comparative religious studies have made in our understanding of the self, Christianity has begun the reconstruction of prayer. If it is true that the self's professions of neighborly love must prove themselves in social deeds, it is also true that the self's professions of loving God must prove themselves in constant prayer. God is the mystery on whom our hearts and minds are set, and prayer is our attending to that mystery.

CONCLUSIONS

The integrity and wisdom that Erikson made the acme of the life cycle are strongly anticipated in contemplative prayer. Prayer, like sleep, "knits up the ravelled sleeve of care" by accomplishing the tranquillity of order. Contemplative prayer is the direct experience that God is not a thing and that love is our treasure. Combined, these can set aright the disordered world view of the contemporary self. As Schumacher put it, we are unhappy because we direct ourselves to trivial things. The overwhelmingly important things are the Mystery which contains our meaning and the loving care which contains our "life." To work in a horizon of love is to restore care, craftsmanship, and creativity. It is to solicit from persons, the soil, and inanimate materials the beauty they long to express.

CHAPTER 5

God

FAITH AND SECULARIZATION

A variety of issues beset the doctrine of God today. There is the question of whether Christian belief, which goes beyond that for which one has certainty, is an ethical act. There is also the question of how much Western technological society militates against the commitment of faith. For those who think of the present age as post-Christian, there is also the question of how to talk of God at all.

Writing largely within a European context, Herbert Vorgrimler[1] indicates three problems that have given rise to "the God question" in modern times. The first is the testimony of numerous persons, both would-be believers and nonbelievers, that they no longer experience God as present. The second derives from the crimes and sufferings (e.g., the holocaust) of this century, which for some persons make the existence of God impossible. Third is that humanity's success, rather than its suffering or powerlessness, renders God unnecessary in explaining the world.

Insofar as "theism" has meant an objective view of God which made God a first cause or first being, it has evoked sophisticated theological critique. In the name of a God above God, or of a demythologized divinity, both Paul

114

Tillich and Rudolf Bultmann tried to bury the anthropomorphic deity of popular imagination.

Some political theologians have put their own accents on this valedictory. Vorgrimler summarizes Dorothee Soelle's views provocatively:

> With the palpable end of the interventions and indeed of the presence of God in history, and with the awareness of the moral postulate of the disappearance of the idea of an Almighty, the end has also come for a theism in which an autonomous God is placed "over there," alien to man.
>
> With this notion of God, the idea of a supernatural and therefore of a prenatal and postmortal existence has disappeared. In Sölle's theology God still has a future. He possesses "as yet unawakened possibilities," he is in the present but only as a *Deus Absconditus,* a "God without qualities."[2]

Soelle finds God in human love, but that just makes the idea of a separate personal God all the more unreasonable to her. The main reason, one suspects, is her fear that those who trust in providence, or pray expecting to be heard, are simply propagating ideology. That is, she suspects they have the sort of mind that supports current human impoverishment.

More positively, other Continental theologians have confronted the testimony to God's absence and responded with what Vorgrimler calls "an enlightened theism." For instance, Helmut Gollwitzer has defended the right of Christian faith to formulate theistic propositions, propositions in which God is the subject of declarative statement, despite the liability of such statements to misinterpretation. Similarly, Heinrich Ott has tried to refine the notion of person so that it can continue to apply to God. In so doing, he has taken a term from trinitarian theology, *perichōrēsis* ("indwelling"), and applied it to the I-Thou encounter between the human self and God. The result is to undercut some of the objections against a personal God "over against" us. Jürgen Moltmann rejects much traditional theism because he feels that the concept of an all-powerful God is out of tune with human suffering, but he wants to retain a suffering God who has personal being in powerlessness and love. Karl Rahner, finally, has labored for a similar renovation of theism in Continental Catholic theology, stressing especially that the experiences of darkness, silence, and God's namelessness orient us to Jesus' cross and resurrection. There, at the cross and resurrection, God appears as a loving reality that metaphysics alone cannot conceive.

Vorgrimler's survey concludes with three assertions that both balance the three problems with which he began and comprehend the overall question that "God" poses today. First, we cannot revise theism or supplant it apart from the vocabulary of the "narrative and faith tradition," the key component of which is the analogous nature of its talk about God. Second, we can only discuss God's attributes successfully if we take great pains to achieve hermeneutical precision. For instance, talk about God's "power" rings differently today when we have seen power's wholesale abuse than it did at the time of the Fourth Lateran Council (1215) or of Vatican I (1869–1870), both of which spoke of "the almighty power of God." Third, we need to take special care in the case of petitionary prayer, where discussions of God's reality often come to acute focus. Two of Vorgrimler's questions show the edge this case wields: "Is God still the God of men when petitionary prayer wholly loses meaning or becomes immanent therapy—mere self-expression? If God is a God who acts as spirit in the spirit of mankind, yet does not interfere in the physical processes of the world (which are under man's control), is it meaningful during a drought to ask for rain?"[3]

Much recent reflection on faith, then, has involved rethinking the modes of God's presence in the world. What does it mean for the "reality" of God that few feel a divine nearness? Similarly, what does it mean that none of the intricate mechanisms of the world that science discovers directly reveals God? Samuel Terrien's *The Elusive Presence* responds to the first point by claiming that the God of biblical faith never was close at hand. If Terrien is correct, biblical religion differed little from our own gropings, and his description sounds quite contemporary:

> In biblical faith, human beings discern that presence is a surging which soon vanishes and leaves in its disappearance an absence that has been overcome. It is neither absolute nor eternal but elusive and fragile, even and especially when human beings seek to prolong it in the form of cultus. The collective act of worship seems to be both the indispensable vehicle of presence and its destroyer. Presence dilutes itself into its own illusion whenever it is confused with a spatial or temporal location. When presence is "guaranteed" to human senses or reason, it is no longer real presence.[4]

Responding to the second point, Charles Birch has effected a gentle debunking of secularists' claims that this is a unique time. Letting a new Job stand for humanity come of scientific age, Birch has God thunder from the whirlwind essentially the same old message:

> Brace yourself like a fighter, for now it is my turn to ask questions and yours to inform me. Where were you at the big bang? How is it that out of a universe of pure hydrogen you have come into existence? Did life begin when the first cell came into existence or do

elements of life exist in the foundations of the universe? How can you be so sure that all life is contrivance? How can mind grow from no mind? Life from nonlife?[5]

Christian faith therefore is far from speechless before contemporary assaults. It can point to a tradition of God's hiddenness, and to the pretentiousness in secularist assumptions that we can put God in the dock. If "God" continues to name the originating and consummating power, the ultimate question of theology, which appears when we understand God's real import, is what God thinks of us. In that sense, biblical faith continues to transcend secularist values.

Against the World

Perhaps expectably, then, theologians of the late '70s are harsh in regard to the quarrels with God which preoccupied their predecessors a decade ago. Neither the death of God nor the life of the secular city wins much of their approval. In the main, current theologians have appropriated enough of Nietzsche and Marx to agree that folk religion often begets alienation. Therefore, they are hard on civil religion that confuses God with Caesar, hard on ecclesiastical religion that confuses God with tradition. Equally, though, they are hard on the facile assumption that secularization has destroyed religion.

A good example of hard-headedness is John Coleman's "Situation for Modern Faith." In it Coleman probes the confusions that afflict recent sociological treatments of religion. His conclusion is worth quoting:

> I have argued for the abandonment of the concept of secularization, because of its conceptual confusion and incoherence, although I hold that some form of the secularization thesis, under careful definition,

may in principle be capable of empirical test. I argue, further, that we replace secularization by an analysis in terms of the individual elements it covers in its catch-all concept. These were seen to be: pluralism; the loss of monopoly control by the churches over other institutional sectors of society and over religion; the rise of individual autonomy in religious matters; privatization and the institutional autonomy of the primary, nonreligious, social sectors.[6]

Among sociologists of religion there is some consensus that the individual elements which "secularization" covers do indeed distinguish present-day faith from its predecessors. On the other hand, there is equal consensus that these individual elements, even conjoined, do not remove what Robert Bellah calls "religious possibility." If there is a tragedy to be read between the lines of Coleman's study, it is that the churches have not exploited this possibility. In somewhat abstract terms, sociologist Guy Swanson voices Coleman's final plea that the churches do better:

> Religious communities must serve to remind all men and all organizations of their mutual incompleteness, to nurture mechanisms and environment in which differences among them can be reconciled if not removed, to witness by their own faithfulness and inner life to the powers possessed by an embodied community, by objective justice and by incarnate charity: the powers to nurture, to elevate, to revive, to renew.[7]

Through the sociology of religion, then, theology recently has updated its old ambivalence toward the world. Immersing itself in both empirical studies of contemporary religion and in sociological theory, much theology now finds both a persistence of religion and a deep suspicion of religion's potential for divorcing human beings from themselves and their world. Perhaps the most dramatic public impact of recent theological concern with such sociology came through the "Hartford Appeal" which Lutherans Peter Berger and Richard John Neuhaus organized. The very title of the book that followed the meetings of their group in 1975 epitomizes the way many "moderates" or "centrists" now feel: *Against the World for the World.* [8]

The core of the Hartford Appeal's concern is the loss of transcendence. It thinks that this loss, manifest in a number of "pervasive themes," debilitates the church's life and work. The themes are: (1) modern thought must be the norm of Christian faith and life; (2) religious statements fall outside reasonable discourse; (3) God is but humanity's noblest creation; (4) contemporary models of humanity must set the terms for our understanding of Jesus; (5) all the religions are equally valid; (6) salvation means realizing one's potential; (7) evil is but the failure to realize potential; (8) the sole purpose of worship is to promote self-realization and human community; (9) authentic religion implies liberation from institutions and historical traditions; (10) the world must set the church's agenda; (11) emphasizing God's transcendence hinders Christian social concern; (12) struggling for a better humanity will bring the Kingdom of God; and (13) hope beyond death is marginal to the Christian understanding of human fulfillment.

The signers of the Hartford Appeal represent the full spectrum of the Christian churches and thus suggest that the themes which the Appeal anathematizes are noxious to all. However, as many "liberal" respondents to the Appeal indicated, it is doubtful that any theologian of moment subscribes to any of the themes as stated, let alone to the full thirteen. It is also doubtful that goodwill could not have shown how many of the themes carry an important and quite orthodox truth. For instance, it is orthodox and true that wrongly emphasizing God's transcendence can hinder social concern. One need go no farther than I John 4:20 to infer that: "If any one says, 'I love God,' and hates his brother, he is a liar; for he who does not love his brother whom he has seen, cannot love God whom he has not seen." It was largely such a wrong emphasis that prompted Marx's famous dictum that religion is the opium of the oppressed. More recently, it has begotten such caveats as Soelle's on prayer. As a matter of empirical observation, prayer *can* become an ideology which diverts people from their tasks in the world. Prayer need not become such an ideology, just as transcendence need not oppose immanence, but both can and have become distorted in these ways.

Of the papers collected in *Against the World for the World,* three are especially interesting. First, Alexander Schmemann's analysis of the Orthodox reaction[9] to the Appeal usefully records Orthodoxy's sense that Hartford merely reiterated its own ancient complaint. The reason for little Orthodox interest in the Hartford Appeal Schemann attributes to its Western origin and orientation. On further reflection, however, he shows that Orthodoxy's contentment to rest outside the Western pale is ill-considered. Indeed, "Western" cultural influences now assault émigré communities as well as those in Greece and Russia. Not to face such influences is to create an illusory sense that older views of the integrity of religion and culture still make Sunday liturgy the center of the workweek.

Schmemann's reflection on Hartford finds vivid exemplification in the record of the discussions which made the Russian Orthodox priest Dmitrii Dudko a household name in Moscow. Focused on parishioners' questions about faith, they show how aggressive Russian scientism and atheism have rendered Christian faith both attractive as well as difficult. The lesson for American theologians is that they can best combat secularism by discerning the idealistic energies it carries and showing that authentic Christian faith is their ally and even their perfector. Thus, *for* the world would become more prominent than *against,* and one would have created an apologetic of encouragement.

A second useful paper is Avery Dulles' "Unmasking Secret Infidelities: Hartford and the Future of Ecumenism." After discussing several sorts of "ecumenism" that Hartford brings to mind, including those of authorship, dialogue, social action, and common witness, Dulles begins his final section by saying: "The effort to grapple with latent heresy is probably the most striking dimension of the ecumenism of the Hartford Appeal." In part, that is because the official ecumenical movement, as represented for instance by the World Council of Churches, largely ignores the task of confronting "the new paganism." Specifically, official ecumenism has not attacked "the rampant immanentism, humanism, secularism, psychologism, sociologism of our age—a convergent movement that leaves no room for the transcendent except as a kind of psychological 'peak experience.' Among recent ecumenical efforts, the Hartford Appeal stands alone in confronting the dominant cultural patterns."[10] Dulles takes pains to stress that the heresies which Hartford attacks are more latent than articulate. He also argues that, far from being an exercise in ecclesiastical triumphalism, Hartford implies that all the churches can themselves threaten Christian faith.

Richard J. Mouw's paper, "New Alignments: Hartford and the Future of Evangelicalism," considers how the concerns of the Appeal tally with what he calls "the thoughts and attitudes of 'conservative-evangelicalism.' "[11] First,

Mouw notes that the conservative organ *Christianity Today* (Feb. 14, 1975) criticized the Hartford statement for saying nothing about the problem of religious authority, that is, for not affirming the full authority and power of the Bible. On the other hand, Mouw himself thinks Hartford brought the discussion of theological specifics much closer to evangelical interests than most ecumenical assemblies do.

To show the possible connections between Hartford and evangelicalism, Mouw has to describe the considerable complexity of the American evangelical scene. In addition to the historical differences among fundamentalists, the pietism of the Jesus People and the charismatics have revived an anti-intellectualism, otherworldliness, and separatism which the neo-evangelical movement has long opposed. Another example of new alignments is the result of the battle among Missouri Synod Lutherans between the Seminex "moderates" and the reigning Preus faction. Whereas *Christianity Today* has supported the latter, "there are many evangelicals who see the Seminex group as engaged in a legitimate struggle against a biblical literalism and an ecclesiastical totalitarianism that are typical of the fundamentalist mentality."[12]

After his description of the current varieties of conservative evangelicalism, Mouw moves to a persuasive analysis of the need for all groups, right and left alike, to criticize their thinking and make it cohere with solid doctrine. In conclusion, he agrees with Wolfhart Pannenberg's assessment of Hartford. Its primary significance resides in its insistence that theological statements are not just reflections of personal preference. Rather, they are directed to the truth, and so are subject to rational criticism.[13] Thus, Hartford should encourage a climate of self-criticism and mutual correction.

RETHINKING GOD

Precisely how the Hartford Appeal will function in the theology of the 1980s is hard to predict, but Peter Berger seems to be a spokesman who is likely to keep its concerns alive. Indeed, Berger seems to enjoy theological polemics, for two years after Hartford he published an article that attacked three prominent "secular theologians." To Schubert Ogden, Berger credited the proposition that faith in God is confidence in life's ultimate worthwhileness. To David Tracy he ascribed the view that, in the dialogue between Christianity and current consciousness, "it is Christianity that must be 'corrected,' and it is the modern spirit that serves as the cognitive instrument for this operation."[14] And in Langdon Gilkey, Berger found the following controversial claim: "The task for twentieth-century Catholicism calls for the reinterpretation of the transcendent, the sacred, the divine—the presence of God to men —into the worldly or naturalistic forms of modern experience rather than in the supernaturalistic forms of Hellenistic and medieval experience."[15] At the end of his essay Berger described the work of these three prominent theologians as having a method whose final cognitive criterion is religious deafness: "When all is said and done, it is a musicology for the deaf."[16]

Eighteen months after Berger's article a vigorous response appeared. None of the three whom Berger had attacked recognized himself in the attacker's description, and each proffered persuasive evidence, from published materials Berger could have consulted, that his "secularism" is more nuanced, and more concerned with preserving the traditional reality of God, than Berger allowed. Keeping to Berger's analogy, Gilkey concluded by shifting key: "May it be, therefore (as a final 'guess'), that the rea-

son for this woeful misreading of my theological texts—as
of those of my two colleagues—is that Berger is 'theologically unmusical'?"[17]

Ogden, Tracy, and Gilkey share membership in the
"Chicago school" of theological studies and an orientation
toward process thought. To my knowledge, the most recent treatment of theology strictly so called by any of
them is Gilkey's new *Message and Existence.*[18]

Gilkey leads into his discussion of God by elucidating the
import of human creatureliness, for such creatureliness
carries a basic sense of God: "Creation as a symbol, therefore, expresses the unconditioned reality and power of
God as the source of all beings, the power grounding all
power, the life from which all life springs, and the eternity
from which time itself originates."[19] However, creation's
relative autonomy, self-direction, and self-constitution
point to a mysterious self-limitation in God: God has cho-
sen to let self-transcending finitudes, creatures, limit his or
her effective absoluteness.

Gilkey advances this description through an analysis of
providence. Providence emphasizes "the relatedness, the
temporality, the conditionedness, and thus the self-limitation of God 'over against' his/her temporal, active, and
autonomous creatures."[20] Thus Gilkey's God combines the
polarities of transcendence and immanence, absoluteness
and relatedness, unconditionedness and conditionedness,
and eternity and temporality. In this it reminds one of
Whitehead's dipolar God.

Gilkey shows quite explicitly how his conception of God
differs from that of classical Christian theology. First, it
affirms potentiality in God and thus an open, undecided
future. Second, it considers God as positively related to the
world and affected by what happens in the world, "by the
story that there unfolds." Third, Gilkey argues from both

God's potentiality and relatedness to the changing world that God shares in creation's temporality and changeability. "God thus 'becomes' as the process becomes, and in this becoming the actuality of God changes."[21]

Positively, such a picture of God squares well with Scripture's descriptions of God as acting in history, as not only related to time and change but sharing in them. Biblical thought did not deprecate history as Hellenistic culture did, and in the process view of God we may well be retrieving the biblical view. Negatively, Gilkey denies that this means ascribing finitude or contingency to God:

> In being affected and related, in changing over time, God is not dependent on other entities or factors for his/her being, nor is he/she correspondingly threatened in his/her being. As the source of all over time —and thus *in* time—God is not contingent but necessary in being; as the uniting principle of past, present, and future—and thus sharing in potentiality—God is infinite.[22]

To handle the conceptual reconciliations that these descriptions imply, Gilkey returns to God's mystery, uniqueness, and holiness. We can only glimpse something of God's transcendence, and something of God's relatedness. However, if we pursue these somethings with the special care that language about God requires, we can forge symbolic language about God that is sufficient for its task.

Much of what Gilkey wants to say about God represents an impressive contemporary consensus. Numerous theologians want to put change, even suffering, at the very core of God's being and love. However, until they can show that such passivity does not make God fall short of our intuitions of perfection and of the Bible's sense of God's complete actuality, there remain good grounds for withholding full assent. It is to Gilkey's credit, however, that he stresses God's *self*-limitation, and so shows us some way out of the dilemma.

A good summary treatment of these philosophical aspects of "God" and of the many others that have arisen historically is Louis Dupré's *The Other Dimension*. [23] Dupré shows the grounds for the historical identification of God with being, and so offers some counterweight to the current tendency to stress divine becoming. He also shows how the dialectical tradition approached God by the negation of being, and how the questions of God's infinity and omnipotence factored in. His treatment is more analytic than constructive, in that no clear personal theology emerges, but it is a salutary reminder that past reflections on God are the sources of most of the difficulties with which recent discussion must deal.

Following Martin Heidegger, John Macquarrie has put forward a useful theology that closely correlates God with being. Though God and being are not identical, the notion that being is "the *incomparable* that *lets-be* and is *present-and-manifest*"[24] allows Macquarrie to make "God" synonymous with "holy being." He underlines that God is not *a* being and works from what he calls an existential-ontological viewpoint, one that is more experiential and concrete than "metaphysics." Macquarrie develops the notion that God does not "exist" but rather "lets-be." Strictly speaking, only *a* being exists, and it would be a reification of God, a transposition of divine Being into the being of a thing, literally to predicate of divinity the sort of standing forth that creatures manifest.

However, this existential-ontological viewpoint does not remove God from creation: "God cannot be conceived apart from the world, for it is of his very essence (letting-be) to create; God is affected by the world as well as affecting it, for creation entails risk and vulnerability; God is in time and history, as well as above them." Thus, Macquarrie's "God" has a twofold meaning. Ontologically, the word denotes Being that is holy and lets-be. Existentially, it expresses an attitude of commitment to, or faith in, being. God's Being includes becoming, for it is God's essence dynamically to let-be. Explicitly, then, Macquarrie too wants to abandon "the traditional 'substantial' (reified) conceptuality in favor of one that takes time and becoming seriously."[25]

EXPERIENCE OF GOD

To what extent is "religious experience" the same as "mystical experience"? That is, to what extent does religious experience imply something extraordinary? A recent volume edited by Steven Katz explores these issues from the standpoint of philosophical analysis. Ninian Smart's contribution, "Understanding Religious Experience," answers the question of religious experience's significance for theology rather grimly, for it both downplays the importance of personal experience of the phenomena that one is studying and postpones the theological evaluation of religious experience to the indefinite future. In support of this second point Smart writes:

> What is often forgotten is that we have a long and delicate path to pick before we are really in a position to make an evaluation; and that path is phenomenological. It means that we must be able to disentangle varieties of religious experience, have a nose for degrees of interpretations in their descriptions, see what they mean existentially, place them in their living contexts and so on. We are still in a very early stage of scientific and human inquiry along these lines, and that inquiry is ill-served if we speed too hastily into questions of theology and evaluation.[26]

Phenomenological religious studies, then, will go slowly in determining how God appears in human lives and what such appearances mean and will prefer scholarship to a quick response to God.

In *The Sense of God,* [27] John Bowker examines the position of contemporary social science on religious experience. In the main, he observes in it a humanist reductionism in that anthropology, sociology, and psychology are at pains to exclude God as the cause of "God." Nonetheless, the data of religious experience do not warrant such a clear conclusion. For all their antiseptic preferences social scientists aware of their work's epistemological complexity have to admit the possibility that an actual deity causes at least some experiences of God.

More recently, in *The Religious Imagination and the Sense of God,* Bowker has studied crises and renewals in the "sense," the convincing experience, of God in late Israelite religion, Jesus, Al Ghazali, and the Buddha. Building on the research of his first volume, he has employed cybernetic theories of information to set such crises and renewals in the context of religious "traditioning," the context of how a people transmits its convictions about God's reality and effects. Somewhat abstractly, Bowker summarizes his results as follows: "The informational point remains the same, that the continuity of a religious tradition depends on the appropriation of what has up to that point been fundamentally resourceful, and on the translation of those resources into the construction of utterance in life." [28] "Resources" in this case means ideas and symbols that give experience coherence sufficient to let life proceed, sufficient, that is, to keep people from a confusion which would impair their ability to act and survive. The "construction of utterance in life" is the articulation of faith which produces such ideas and symbols.

This applies to religious experience, and to how theology ought to regard religious experience, because the primary "translation" of traditional resources occurs in prayer. Indeed, prayer is the source of a tradition's informational cues: "So to rest and move and live within the disposition and intention of our brain behaviour, that we —the very subject of that behaviour—are moved beyond the inherited point of our departure into a new and volunteered dependence—until, indeed, we realize in ourselves the meaning of Augustine's otherwise quite unverifiable assertion, 'God is the only reality, and we are only real in so far as we are in his order, and he in us.' "[29] In other words, it is direct contact with its ultimate reality that keeps any religious tradition alive. If so, phenomenological hedging of the reality of such an "ultimate reality," the refusal to evaluate the ground to which religious experience points, means such a diminution of what those who have religious experiences say "appears" to them that the data are radically distorted.

For theology, God is reality so necessary to human meaning and value that one can never avoid the possible divinity of any human experience. Theology should stand for scholarship subordinate to the practical, existential need all people, including theologians, have to make sense of the mystery which governs their daily lives. Thus, the utility of a theology which does not believe in mystery, or does not care to let the reality of mystery guide its scholarship, is limited indeed.

Raimundo Panikkar epitomizes in his autobiography many of the tensions which beset Christian theologizing about non-Christian religious experience. In his more recent *The Intrareligious Dialogue*[30] he condemns Christian provincialism, argues passionately against the detachment characteristic of phenomenological religious studies, and demonstrates the riches awaiting those willing to dialogue with non-Christian religious experience in an existential way.

Panikkar introduces his argument with a distinction between faith and belief that is essential to understanding intrareligious dialogue:

> The distinction between faith and belief, along with the thesis that faith is a constitutive human dimension, represents more than just an intellectual venture. It is equally an existential adventure: a human pilgrimage within religious traditions divided by multisecular walls of history, philosophies, theologies, and prejudices.

In his own case, this distinction was crucial. Born in India of Hindu and Christian parents, he studied in Europe and then went back to India. When he was on a return trip to Europe, friends asked how he was faring. His reply was:

> Although my human pilgrimage was not yet finished, I used to give a straightforward—obviously incomplete—answer: I "left" as a Christian, I "found" myself as a Hindu and I "return" a Buddhist, without having ceased to be a Christian. Some people nevertheless wonder whether such an attitude is objectively tenable or even intelligible. Here is a reply in outline that I hope will also throw some light on the spiritual condition of humankind today—even if it belongs to my historical past.[31]

As one might expect, his personal experience gives Panikkar a dour view of most Western ecumenism. In practice, it restricts the *significantly* "inhabited world" to that which shares its own basic culture. The rest of the world's cultures it considers simply fields to which to transplant Western faith. As with other Western exports, this risks disrupting other cultures' ecologies:

The great temptation for ecumenism is to extrapolate —to use a native growth beyond the bounds of its native soil. We have seen what comes of exporting European and American democracy; we know that the baffling population explosion over much of the world's surface comes of exporting antibiotics, DDT and the like. No one-way movement—certainly not exporting a gospel—can solve our present problems. I do not for a moment suggest that there be no crossing of borders. I am only saying that most solutions to our problems remain terribly provincial; we do not yet have categories adequate to the exigencies of our *kairos.*[32]

What does this demand of us? At the least, it demands that we let other religionists speak in their own language. In living Asian religion, *tao* is not just a "way"; *Brahman* is significantly different from "God," *atman* is more than "soul," *dharma* means something other than "justice," and *chan* conveys things "meditation" cannot. For Panikkar this implies a greater respect for a different style of dialogue than Western theology has preferred. Panikkar, speaking metaphorically, has "province" stand for narrowness of mind, and by contrast, "parish" stand for homey, down-to-earth, regional matters. The difference is that "parish," for all its particularity, remains open:

> From the steeple of the parish church many other steeples can be seen. A theological hermeneutic of this symbol tells us that the parish will be whole only when the Pantocrator, the Lord of all the universe, is at its center and there holds communion (this is the right word) for the whole world. . . . The identity our age so frantically seeks is not individuality (which ends in solipsism), not generality (which ends in alienation), but the awareness of that constitutive relativity

which makes of us but connections in the mysterious warp and woof of being.[33]

In the last sentence Panikkar is in a Hindu mood. From both family life and professional encounters, he has learned Hindu philosophies of being, as he has felt the equivalence of Christ and Krishna. Why? At least in part because of what they mean to those with whom he has dialogued:

> The Krsna of our dialogue is not a historical or mythological figure but the Krsna of faith, of my interlocutor's personal faith. His belief is the one I must assume, sharing his truth, the truth of the Krsna of faith.[34]

Without such an assumption, one can never appreciate what Krishna really means to a devout Vaishnavite Hindu, and without such meaning Christians will never attain the full *growth* they might. Indeed, the dialogue that true encounter of the religions, encounter from their respective living centers of faith, anticipates "stands on the assumption that nobody has access to the universal horizon of human experience, and that only by not postulating the rules of the encounter from a single side can Man proceed toward a deeper and more universal understanding of himself and thus come closer to his own realization."[35]

The implication of this for future Christian theology is that it must take seriously, as a stimulus to rethinking its own doctrine of God, such non-Christian symbols of ultimacy as absolute *Brahman* the impersonal and *Sunyata* the final emptiness. No longer can dialogue among the world's religions remain a matter simply of translating other beliefs into one's own terms, of using, for instance, one's own God as the sole criterion of other religious experiences.

FEMINIST REFLECTION ON GOD

Beyond Androcentrism, edited by Rita Gross, conjoins feminist reflection on religious realities with general studies in world religions. Thus, it gives some indication of what scholars liberated from the traditional male roles and values might achieve. A study by Gael Hodgkins, for instance, shows how having a female divinity, the goddess Sedna, affects the sense of the transcendent of some religious Eskimos. Similarly, a study by Joanna Rodgers Macy shows how *Prajnaparamita,* the Buddhist Perfection of Wisdom, has a maternal aspect.[36] Studies elsewhere by historians of religions show the power of female divinity symbolized in the Bodhisattva Kuan-yin, the Chinese Tao, and various Hindu deities.[37] Evidence is thus accumulating that other cultures have incorporated feminine experience into their "theology" better than Western Christian culture has. If intrareligious dialogue is to influence future Christian theology, one should expect the femininity of God to be a constant feature.

Judith Plaskow's "The Feminist Transformation of Theology" dates the beginning of contemporary feminist theology to 1960, with the publication of Valerie Goldstein's article, "The Human Situation: A Feminist View." Plaskow summarizes its significance as follows:

> Goldstein set out—at least implicitly—what were to become the two basic tenets of all feminist theology: first, theology, whether it recognizes it or not, is rooted in the particularities of human experience, including the theologian's experience as male or female. Second, theology has in fact been rooted in

male experience in such a way as, on the one hand, to ignore women's experience, and on the other hand, to reinforce a very traditional conception of women's nature and role.[38]

Goldstein attacks this latter in the theology of Reinhold Niebuhr and Anders Nygren, arguing that their equation of sin with pride and self-centeredness fails to apply to women whose sins result from a lack of personal pride and an underdeveloped or negative self-image.

In Plaskow's opinion, the first wave of feminist theology after Goldstein has been successful in exposing the relationship between traditional theology's understandings of God and human nature and its depreciating views of women. Plaskow doubts, however, that feminist theology to date has conceived women's experience broadly enough to serve as a foundation for a more general theological scheme. Rather, feminist theology often

has forgotten that women's experience is as diverse and complex as the experience of the human race. Naomi Goldenberg, in the first draft of her thesis, shows very nicely how in Daly's *Beyond God the Father,* the experience of nothingness opens into an experience of sisterhood which is in many respects quite coercive. Women's experience of our failures and evasions, our collusion with a patriarchal system, our own capacity for evil is relegated to the past, swept aside in a great "hoorah" for the transforming power of sisterhood.[39]

Plaskow's agenda for feminist theology, then, involves taking seriously everything that reflects women's experience authentically. She hopes thereby to short-circuit premature universalizing. Further, her agenda involves facing more pointedly the fact that theology involves talking about a reality not defined by our experiences, regardless of our genders.

The resulting sketch of theology is persuasive because it gives both empirical and transcendent explanations of religious experience their due. As feminist, Plaskow's theology must remain in touch with women's particular experiences, while as theological, it must reach out to God and God's universality. This means neither pretending to speak for God nor abandoning the specific culture in which the experiences that occasion theology occur. It does mean forcing theology to recognize the existence and validity of women's experience.

Phyllis Trible's recent *God and the Rhetoric of Sexuality*[40] shows that a significant amount of female imagery occurs in the biblical texts, if one but has an eye to see.

The male and female metaphorical images of God lead Trible to study the womb as a metaphor for divine compassion. This in turn brings to light further images of God as one who conceives, is pregnant, writhes in labor pains, brings forth a child, and nurses. Confident that the femininity of God is recognized in the Bible, Trible examines the tragic disobedience that shattered full communion of the sexes in Genesis 2 to 3, the innocent eroticism of the Song of Songs, and the daily struggle for existence of biblical women as exemplified by Ruth. In each case, the Bible says more positive things about women's experience than later Christian theology does.

Trible's exegesis of the Genesis account of human sexuality (Gen. 2:21–24) shows that "woman is no weak, dainty, ephemeral creature. No opposite sex, no second sex, no derived sex—in short, 'no Adam's rib.' Instead, woman is the culmination of creation, fulfilling humanity in sexuality." Her reading of the Song of Songs produces the same evaluation: "There is no male dominance, no female subordination, and no stereotyping of either sex. Specifically, the portrayal of the woman defies the connotations of 'second sex.' She works, keeping vineyards and pasturing flocks. Throughout the Song she is independent, fully the equal of the man."[41]

Concerning The Book of Ruth, Trible finds that the women whom the story depicts, Naomi and Ruth, work out their own salvation confident that God works in them. Naomi is traditional, though not rigidly so, while "Ruth and the females of Bethlehem work as paradigms for radicality."[42] Together, they show biblical women as part of patriarchal culture but also as transforming it. Thus, as an intrinsic part of the human image of God and as source of transformation, biblical woman sustains Scripture as the word of a creative, ever-new God.

CHAPTER 6

Christology

METHOD

Because Jesus Christ is the center of Christianity, Christology is the center of Christian theology. Both historically and theologically, there would be no Christian religion had not Jesus of Nazareth lived, worked, died, and been raised.

Thinking about Jesus, of course, leads to the New Testament, where the most original data about Jesus lie, and to historical, linguistic, sociological, and other studies that serve to develop our thinking about Jesus. However, Scripture is not an unambiguous source. As David Kelsey's *The Uses of Scripture in Recent Theology* shows, theologians read Scripture in accord with their own image of Christian reality: "It is that imaginative characterization of the central reality of Christianity, 'what it is finally all about,' that *is* decisive for the way the theologian actually construes and uses biblical texts as scripture in the course of doing theology."[1] Kelsey places theologians within the familiar hermeneutical circle: they get their sense of Christian reality in part from the way Scripture is used in church life, in liturgy, for instance, and they use this sense itself as an interpretational key to Scripture.

This problem figures also in Edward Schillebeeckx' *Jesus: An Experiment in Christology.* Schillebeeckx makes the believer's quest for salvation the place where Jesus becomes decisive. At the same time, he makes Jesus the criterion of salvation, the norm of wholeness and health: "For the Christian, Jesus—whom he encounters in his experience as the final source of salvation—is of course the final criterion."[2]

Other theologians share Schillebeeckx' interest in both contemporary Christian experience and historical Christianity. Julian Hartt's *Theological Method and Imagination* combines an appreciation of both contemporary consciousness and Scripture's perennial authority.

> What is coveted there is an authority that is both inexpungable and assimilable to the quotidian world. The latter is as important as the former because it marks a refusal to let even God's truth rend the fabric of daily existence. Indeed no such possibility is acknowledged, even in the abstract. But in that case, what is the inexpungable authority of the Bible? Just this: In what Scripture says about salvation it is not to be doubted. Moreover, what Scripture says about salvation, its conditions, and its effects (and its affects), is full of practical value for rightly ordering life in the here and now.[3]

Biblical scholars themselves struggle inordinately with questions of method. Though primarily linguists and historians, their constant association with Scriptural texts forces them to attend constantly to questions of source and significance. In the introduction to his *Jesus and the Language of the Kingdom,* the late Norman Perrin listed the hermeneutical levels which the biblical scholar uncovers. First, there is the task of textual criticism to establish the text itself. Second is historical criticism to discover the author's circumstances and original intent. Third, beyond historical criticism lies literary criticism, concern "with the nature and natural force of both the literary form and language of a text."[4] Last is the act of interpretation itself. Perrin derives from Bultmann an overrrriding interest in the dynamic interaction between the text and its interpreter. The interpreter questions the text for its understanding of human existence, but the text in turn questions the interpreter's own understanding.

This is not to say that all biblical scholars follow the hermeneutical process to an existential conclusion. When introducing an issue of the *Journal of the American Academy of Religion* devoted to New Testament interpretation from the perspective of process theology, John Cobb and others felt it necessary to say that "most Biblical scholars, like historians generally, find it possible to go on with their work without troubling much about theological or philosophical matters. They see no reason to bother with this discussion until and unless it speaks directly to their historical concerns. . . . Any form of systematic theology is fundamentally truncated where its rootage in Scripture is not clear and strong. Although the rootage of process theology in Scripture is real it is insufficiently manifest and is in danger of further withering if it cannot be articulated and integrated with creative contemporary Biblical scholarship."[5]

Precisely how to bring about this articulation and integration remains elusive, for with rare exceptions neither theologians nor exegetes share one another's gifts. To collaborate in terms of functionally related specialties they would have to share a common view of the theological enterprise, but at the moment, such sharing seems far away. As Cobb puts it: "The separation of theology from Biblical studies is only one expression of the ever-increasing fragmentation of academic disciplines in general and especially of the growing disconnection of historical scholarship from normative thinking."[6]

Bernard Lonergan has recently paid special attention to the problems of method in Christology, in a critical review of Piet Schoonenberg's *The Christ.* For Lonergan, the theologian constantly faces in Christology the question of how to select "what is valid in current views without becoming involved in positions open to radical change."[7] A first answer to this is that current historical studies are more successful in describing the beliefs of the early church than they are in reconstructing the Jesus of history. Thus, at the present time the theologian ought to concentrate on the structure and intelligibility of the early church's beliefs about Jesus rather than on Jesus as a historical person.

Further, Christological method should make possible a Christology that is both functional (concerned with Christ's works) and ontological (concerned with Christ's being). Finally, Christology must clarify its methodology by examining its own heuristic or anticipatory structure: "A heuristic structure is a conjunction both of data on the side of the object and of an operative criterion on the side of the subject."[8] The object is Jesus. The subject is the inquirer, the theologian. Christologies have historically made use of this heuristic structure.

On the side of the subject the heuristic structure poses such questions as, How are we to understand Jesus as Son of God? Does his title mean, "as the Church for centuries has understood it, that Jesus was truly a man leading a truly human life but his identity was the identity of the eternal son of God consubstantial with the Father"? The answer Lonergan offers is our experience of the Spirit, for the Spirit allows us to discern what the world cannot. Indeed, "it is in the progressive clarification of Christian

experience and in the continuous exercise of spiritual dis-
cernment in the Christian community that christological
doctrine developed."⁹ Our task today is to bring our understanding of Jesus up to the expectations of hermeneutics, history, psychology, and critical philosophy.

Lonergan believes we can accomplish this and breathe
fresh life into old doctrines without destroying traditional
dogma. He believes, for instance, that we can develop a
doctrine of the hypostatic union to meet the objection that
there being only one person in Jesus, that of the divine
Word, would destroy his humanity. As may be clear by the
end of this chapter, current hermeneutics can only with
difficulty sustain Chalcedon's classic pronouncements on
the humanity and divinity of Christ. Lonergan's modesty
about altering tradition reflects the First Vatican Council's
reservations about the ability of speculative theology to
penetrate divine mystery.

RECENT NEW TESTAMENT TRENDS

A readable overview of recent New Testament theology
is Stephen Neill's *Jesus Through Many Eyes.* On the problem of discerning a single New Testament theology in the
diversity of the New Testament canon, Neill says:

> Each of these traditions is a reflection, or a shadow, of
> the Christ. Can we pass beyond the differences in the
> various accounts to find an underlying unity of event
> that has given rise to them all? . . . How near can we
> come to seeing him not just through the eyes of many
> beholders but as he was in the simple majesty of his
> historical existence? This is the question that, sooner
> or later, every theology of the New Testament must
> face.¹⁰

Neill believes that radical skepticism about the details of Jesus' life and teaching ended with Ernst Käsemann's new quest for the historical Jesus. Since then scholars have come to agree on the distinctiveness of Jesus' parables, the centrality of the Kingdom of God in the preaching of Jesus, and the antiquity of the passion narratives. There is also agreement that the devotion of Jesus to God his "Father," his call for repentance and forgiveness, his clear sense of mission, his confidence that God is gracious love, his sense of standing in a crucial "end" time, and his willingness to suffer for his message unto death were probably also historically the case.

Because the majority of New Testament studies are by Christians, one gains a new angle of vision from studies of Jesus such as that of Géza Vermès, *Jesus the Jew.* In the first part Vermès deals with "the setting," the Jewish, Galilean, and charismatic elements in the history of the period. The second part concerns the New Testament titles of Jesus. In conclusion, Vermès offers a brief review of his findings:

> Without doubt, it is that whereas none of the claims and aspirations of Jesus can be said definitely to associate him with the role of Messiah, not to speak of that of *son of man,* the strange creation of the modern myth-makers, everything combines, when approached from the viewpoint of a study of first-century A.D. Galilee, or of charismatic Judaism, or of his titles and their development, to place him in the venerable company of the Devout, the ancient Hasidim. Indeed, if the present research has any value at all, it is in this conclusion that it is most likely to reside, since it means that any new enquiry may accept as its point of departure the safe assumption that Jesus did not belong among the Pharisees, Essenes, Zealots or

Gnostics, but was one of the holy miracle-workers of Galilee.[11]

This is not to say that Vermès tames Jesus by categorizing him. On the contrary, Vermès speaks of "the incomparable superiority of Jesus" to other ancient Hasidim, and he quotes Klausner's judgment of Jesus: "In his ethical code there is a sublimity, distinctiveness and originality in form unparalleled in any other Hebrew ethical code; neither is there any parallel to the remarkable art of his parables."[12] Vermès sees in Jesus profundity of insight, grandeur of character, and unsurpassed mastery of the inmost core of spiritual truth, the existential relationship of human beings to one another and to God.

Vermès thinks Jesus' own claims rather modest when compared to the titles accorded him by his followers. Unwilling to accept the modest historical meaning of the evangelists' words, Christian orthodoxy's doctrinal structure is based on an arbitrary interpretation of the sayings of Jesus recorded in the New Testament. Christian New Testament scholars are thus today somewhat skeptical about the historical authenticity of these sayings. By contrast, Vermès finds in Jesus "Jesus the just man, the *zaddik*, Jesus the helper and healer, Jesus the teacher and leader, venerated by his intimates and less committed admirers alike as prophet, lord and *son of God.*"[13]

Vermès represents the culture "outside" Christianity with which Christian theology ought constantly to be in dialogue. Even further outside is Milan Machoveč's *A Marxist Looks at Jesus.*[14] Machoveč, a Czech, participated in the dialogue between Marxists and Christians at Marienbad before the Russian invasion of Czechoslovakia in August of 1968. From that dialogue, he became convinced that Christians and Marxists have things to offer one another, not the least of which might be interpretations of Jesus.

Humanistically, Machoveč finds an overwhelming personality behind the teachings of Jesus. People were amazed at his *authority,* as in Mark 1:22. People flocked to Jesus because he exemplified the Kingdom. Politically, Jesus' message and personality alike drew upon the suffering of his people, and he exemplified many of their ardent hopes for a new order. In Machoveč's interpretation, the Kingdom of God that Jesus preached is the change tomorrow begs of today. Repentance and conversion mean to "change your minds, become different." The central teaching of Jesus is, thus, that "all subsequent details possess authenticity only to the extent that we understand them as the details of a basic message concerning repentance for the Kingdom of God."[15]

Such repentance Machoveč contrasts with "the conventional popular-prophetic picture" and with popular fantasy about the end of the world. Jesus insisted that the future was humanity's concern in the here and now, and it could be only what they made of the present. This allies Jesus to Marx:

> Jesus gives this future dimension its human character by ridding it of its alienated, apocalyptic and fantastic character and liberating it from the prison of metaphysics. Jesus in this way abolishes the future as something that merely replaces the present, a wretched, lost, squandered future, a future in which the prevailing misery of human reality is met only by empty dreams. Jesus shows not how to escape from the misery of real life but how to overcome one's own moral misery and lowliness.[16]

Intrinsic to this was Jesus' critique of his own culture, expressed in denunciation of the wealthy and powerful and praise for the poor and the outcast. Against the Pharisees, Jesus demanded that one be *oneself* the means of social revolution. The tragedy of Christianity, as Machoveč sees it, is that the revolutionary Jesus was supplanted by a supernatural one. The Marxist humanist and the true follower of Jesus have in common hope for the future and a radical commitment to justice.

An attractive reflection on Jesus' personality that situates him against the background of the Old Testament is Lucas Grollenberg's *Jesus*. Grollenberg is interested in Jesus the man and distrustful of emphasizing the divinity of Christ and other features of a Christology "from above." Thus, though he writes from within Christian faith, his accents are similar to those of Vermès and Machoveč. For instance, Grollenberg spotlights the Jesus who took to heart the biblical belief in God's love:

> Jesus believed that the God of Israel wrote no one off or, in positive terms, that the mystery denoted by the word "God" is a love which goes out to everyone and seeks to embrace all men. He felt himself called, "elected" to express this love and to make it a decisive factor in human relationships. That was what God had always intended. Israel had been chosen to carry out his plan and now Jesus was taking the task upon himself. He felt that he had been called to serve all mankind.[17]

Jesus' attitudes were founded on Hosea's depiction of God's constancy despite Israel's infidelity, Second Isaiah's and the psalmist's confidence in God's dominion over history, and the prophets' demands for justice. The God of tradition Jesus inherited was a God of pure goodness who evoked love. Later Israelite religion forsook this love for history and law. Similarly, later generations took the New

Testament's subjective reminiscences of Jesus for literal reports.

For Grollenberg, the person who elicited the reminiscences of the New Testament moved in an atmosphere of trust. This derived from Jesus' complete confidence in God his father and he extended it to all the people he met. The energies people normally. invest in self-defense became free for service, and Jesus showed what could happen when people gave themselves wholly to "God." Grollenberg seems to say that Jesus was the son of God because he was extraordinarily human.

J. L. Houlden's study, *Ethics and the New Testament,*[18] lacks Grollenberg's personalism but is alike in its estimate of Jesus. Houlden suggests that it was the extraordinary and religiously deviant freedom Jesus felt from the law that brought about his death. He was so overwhelmed by God's presence and by the approach of the Kingdom that he felt himself free from the law. In its place he provided an ethic of response to God and recognition of neighbor. New Testament ethics tried simply to preserve the views for which Jesus ultimately gave his life.

Scholars who have taken part in the new quest for the historical Jesus, whatever their ideological point of departure, agree about his extraordinary humanity. They may not retain those theological doctrines which would support claims to divinity, but by means of historical methodology they reconstruct a personality powerful and authoritative enough to account for the historical impact of Christianity.

The Parables

Recent scholarship especially prizes the parables as helpful to a historical reconstruction of Jesus. Norman Perrin's *Jesus and the Language of the Kingdom* describes scholarship's steady progress in studying the parables. In recent years, the foremost work has been done in the United States by Amos Wilder, Robert Funk, Dan Via, and John Dominic Crossan. All use common literary critical tools. These complement historical techniques such as redaction criticism, the analysis of a text's editorial history, and thereby circumvent some of the limitations of historical analysis. Via has noted that historical approaches to the parables suffer because we cannot pinpoint their context in Jesus' life. They tend also to ignore the parables' basic humanity and their aesthetic nature and function.[19]

John Dominic Crossan, whom Perrin considers to be currently the most influential theorist, approaches the parables as poetic metaphors. This enables him to distinguish parable from allegory:

> Crossan is developing an argument to the effect that the Parables of Jesus contrast with allegory as symbol contrasts with allegory in the eyes of the poets, and as myth contrasts with allegory in the eyes of Paul Ricoeur. Parable, like symbol, expresses what cannot be expressed in another way, demands a "right instinct" for understanding, partakes of the reality it renders intelligible, and invites participation in its referent. Parable, like myth, reveals something not reducible to a clear language. Allegory, by contrast, expresses what can and should be expressed in another way; it demands a "right knowledge" for understanding; it is an abstraction from reality; it intends to convey a point in intellectual terms; it can be abandoned when its message has been grasped.[20]

From an analysis of the parables of the hidden treasure (Matt. 13:44), the pearl of great price (Matt. 13:45–46), and the great fish (Apocryphal Gospel of Thomas 81:28 to 82:3), Crossan thinks he can structure the whole message of Jesus in terms of advent, reversal, and action.

In his own discussion of the parables of the Kingdom, Perrin insists first that they show the Kingdom to be a symbol of God acting as king. Second, they heighten the drama of the Kingdom's approach because of their enigmatic language. A master of metaphor, Jesus used language that would shock his hearers out of their complacency with a new vision of the world.

After Perrin, William Beardslee has contrasted the parable with enigmatic literary forms such as the proverb and the koan, and explored some of their philosophical implications. Despite technical differences, parables, proverbs, and koans are alike in their literary and psychological dynamics. In the proverbs of the desert fathers, for instance, one sees an effort to unite the hearer to the mysterious otherness of the divinity. The intuition that divine transcendence is, for us, largely negative implies both God's darkness and our ignorance. The Zen koan, like the proverb, forces those who take it seriously to understand beyond conceptions, from the heart. Ultimately, enlightenment, realization, and the Buddhist *satori* imply restructuring one's consciousness, even one's whole personality.[21]

Beardslee's most intriguing observations deal with the reasons why the parables dominate current scholarship, and what this implies for traditional Christian faith and its dialogue with other religions. On current scholarship he writes: "It was not only a better perception of the form of the parables, but also—perhaps at a fundamental level even more—a loss of participation in the story of salvation which led . . . to the abandonment of . . . earlier, somewhat naive interpretation of the parables." More precisely, the current stress on discontinuity reflects "a quest for interpretation of the gospels and of Jesus that will be viable in a world which does not find the testable or commonly-experienced continuities of life to be transparent to the Spirit or the divine."[22]

This leads Beardslee to the negative aspect of divine mystery. To do justice to Jesus' message, theology must keep in mind the concept of the divine nothingness. Beardslee thinks that a process ontology can give mystery its due.[23] The result is a sketch of how New Testament studies, philosophy, and interreligious dialogue might cooperate. Though there are other promising areas of New Testament research, Christology has much to gain from current studies of the parables.

SYSTEMATIC STUDIES

Lewis Ford's *The Lure of God* begins by denying that any "high" Christology is possible in a process perspective: "Is it possible for the divine subjectivity to become actualized in some way within the man Jesus? Our answer is negative, for none of the alternatives seem to work. Either we adopt a social trinity in which only one of several divine subjectivities becomes incarnate, or the one and only subjectivity of God is realized in Jesus."[24] Both alternatives are unacceptable, so from the outset Jesus is not regarded as divine, and cannot be the locus of God's becoming human. Rather, we must distinguish between the Logos, which designates the totality of God's creative aims, and the Christ, who signifies God's purpose in salvation. In this way, we avoid the classical problem of how Christ can be both fully human and fully divine.

On the resurrection, Ford holds that the body that is resurrected is the church: "We argue for the bodily resurrection of Christ, but the body of Christ's resurrection is none other than the body of Christ which is the church, understood as that emergent community of love guided by the dynamic activity of Christ's Spirit. According to Luke and Paul, Simon Peter was the first person to form that body whose mind is the risen Christ, thereby effecting the bodily resurrection."[25] This seems to take us rather far from Jesus, but it does echo Paul's interest in the organic unity and new life of the followers of Jesus.

Finally, Ford is concerned to show that the cross symbolizes reconciliation, God's willingness to transform the evil of the world. "He stands ready to receive into his own being all the evil of the world to bring about its transformation, and this experience of evil is the divine suffering epitomized by the crucifixion. This is the most profound manifestation of the presence of the consequent nature in our experience."[26] The crucifixion shows God powerless and unable to comfort Jesus, his beloved. Jesus died that the Christ could be born.

Ford's analyses show what the steady application of process convictions may produce, but by his own admission, they are quite different from the faith of Nicaea, Chalcedon, and Ephesus.

In *Jesus the Christ*, Walter Kasper posed the tasks in Christology for the contemporary theologian. The first is to produce an interpretation of Jesus that fits the facts of his life and times as the best historical research establishes them. Second, an adequate contemporary Christology must be "universally responsible." By this Kasper seems to mean that it must make what it says about Jesus relevant to the questions people ask about their lives. Third, and most important, a contemporary Christology must be about salvation. Kasper argues: "We know the nature of a thing only by way of its appearance: from, that is, its being for another, and therefore from its meaning for, and effect on, an other. The actual meaning of a profession of faith in Jesus Christ and of Christological teaching is only apparent if we inquire into the liberating and redemptive meaning of Jesus."[27]

To satisfy those requirements, Kasper focuses on (1) Jesus' history, (2) the basis and content of faith in Jesus' resurrection, and (3) Jesus' mystery. In the final portion of his work, where he discusses mediatorship, Kasper judges the dogma of Chalcedon to be a precise version in the language of its time of what the New Testament says we encounter in Jesus. Similarly, he judges any Christology that proceeds purely "from below" a failure, because Jesus understood himself "from above." And finally, Kasper defends the doctrine of the hypostatic union of divinity and humanity in Jesus as "a conceptual, ontological expression of the Biblical statement that God has manifested himself in Jesus Christ as love."[28]

On the road to such final statements, Kasper tries to update Christological doctrine and make it credible to his contemporaries. His defense of the conciliar teachings is neither conservative nor uncritical. But his obvious effort to theologize within the tradition makes Kasper's emphasis on soteriology all the more impressive.

Hans Küng's best-selling *On Being a Christian* shares Kasper's interest in soteriology without, however, sharing its studied attention to the conciliar past. Küng's accent is the Christological present, the interest in Jesus that our contemporaries, Christian or not, manifest. If the really distinctive feature of Christianity is precisely the Jesus from whom it derives, then Christology is the core of being a Christian. To search out the real Christ, it follows, will be an act of apologetics in the most acceptable sense.

"Everything can be called Christian which in theory and practice has an explicit, positive reference to Jesus Christ."[29] But to which Christ are we to refer? There is the Christ of piety, the Christ of dogma, and the Christ of literature. None of them, for Küng, is what we finally seek. Rather, the real Christ is Jesus of Nazareth, the first-century Jew to whom historical investigation gives us some access. Consequently, Küng's major interest is to reconstruct what he can of Jesus' "program." This entails trying to answer two historical questions: Who is Jesus? and, What did he want?

Küng proceeds by eliminating the options Jesus had available. Thus, Jesus chose to be neither priest nor theologian. He stood neither with the rulers of his time nor with the revolutionaries who wanted to overthrow them. He was neither a monk nor an ascetic, neither devout nor legalistic like the Pharisees. Küng's opinion is that Jesus' program was total subordination to his cause. "And what is this cause? It can be described in one sentence: *Jesus' cause is the cause of God in the world.* It is fashionable now to insist that Jesus is wholly and entirely concerned with man. This is true. But he is wholly and entirely concerned with man because he is first of all wholly and entirely concerned with God."[30]

The central expression of Jesus' cause was his preaching of the Kingdom. Insofar as the Kingdom represented God's will, preaching it also promoted "man's cause," for Jesus thought that the fundamental transformation which human beings need would come from surrender to God's will.

Another expression of Jesus' program was love. God consistently wills humanity's well-being. Jesus loved the handicapped of his day, the sick, the "possessed," women, children, and the poor. This partiality led him into conflict with the prevailing powers, who could not accept his radical advocacy of the have-nots. What sustained Jesus in this conflict was his intimacy with God his Father. Indeed, he expressed God's own advocacy and initiative unforgettably in the parable of the prodigal son. For the early Christians, the way that people responded to Jesus the advocate was identical to their response to God, for Jesus was a perfect witness to the ultimate source of our grace and love. Küng in this way affirms Jesus' divine Sonship.

In retrospect, the fate of this man so close to the source of grace seems almost inevitable. "Only a complete rethinking, a real *metanoia* on the part of those affected, a new awareness, an abandonment of preoccupation with their own activity, giving up all legalistic self-assurance and self-justification, and a return to radical trust in the God of unconditional grace and abounding love proclaimed by Jesus could have averted this disaster."

Küng treats the resurrection as an act of God, not historical in the strict sense. It is not really imaginable, but nonetheless it occurs, in the sense that the personal reality of Jesus remains and is even completed. From the resurrection, Christians derive their conviction that "death is not destruction but metamorphosis—not a diminishing but a finishing."[31]

The Easter message therefore is essentially the proclamation that Jesus died and was taken up into God's own primordial life. For primitive faith, Christ crucified and raised is the axis and basic criterion of Christian existence. Küng labors to pay later dogmatic interpretations of Jesus their due, but the preponderance of scriptural materials he gives shows that the heart of his book is a description of the earliest Christian faith. In the pages of *On Being a Christian,* Jesus is a most remarkable, attractive, profound human being.

The Christology of Karl Rahner's *Foundations of Christian Faith* begins with our present evolutionary view of the world. To communicate successfully with our contemporaries, Rahner thinks, we must make

sense of the Logos' incarnation in the world science
now describes. From this beginning Rahner then moves
through nine other issues, including what it means to
say "God became man," how we are to understand
Jesus' life, death, and resurrection, and how both classical and recent Christologies now stand.

The crux of Rahner's argument, in my view, is the notion of absolute savior, a contemporary rendering of the
dogma of the hypostatic union of God and man in Christ.
But whereas the traditional notion tended to view the
divine and human natures as extrinsic, the notion of the
absolute savior does justice to the interior issues which
modern reflection raises. It also does justice to our present
conviction that only parable and poetic speech humanize
divine mystery.

"Absolute savior" is an extrapolation of what humanity
and the world need if they are to fulfill their dynamic
natures in union with God. From the "below" of what we
are and of how our world is constituted, the "absolute
savior" emerges as the personal place where the Mystery
that sponsors our hopes itself fulfills them. Thus, the "absolute savior" provides both "salvation" and "eschaton," the
healing of ourselves and our world for which our hearts
long.

Rahner would be the last person to deny that this extrapolation from the below of our human natures and
world is not made possible by Christian faith. He is very
candid that his analyses of the human condition and the
evolutionary world process are enlightened and guided by
the gospel. Further, he believes that this work from below
is raised up by the above that faith finds in Jesus. As divine
Logos, Jesus is precisely God's trinitarian self-expression
come into our midst. As the Word for which we listen in
the core of our beings, his presence in our midst is grace,

salvation, and eschatological fulfillment. In Jesus, then, above and below are united.

The Resurrection

In both systematic and biblical Christologies, the resurrection stands out as the problem discussed most vigorously in recent writings. Edward Schillebeeckx is the systematician most thoroughly immersed in current biblical criticism, and it is a sorry irony that his *Jesus* should have been an occasion of ecclesiastical controversy. Schillebeeckx has devoted considerable space to studies of the Gospels as general interpretations of the risen Jesus and direct interpretation of the resurrection in the New Testament. We can only hint at the richness of these studies, but perhaps this will provoke some readers to take up *Jesus* for themselves.

On general interpretation, Schillebeeckx thinks that the New Testament best presents Jesus' resurrection in its accounts of his historical message, ministry, "mighty works," dealing with people, and manner of living and dying. It was not the prevailing Jewish apocalyptic that motivated the New Testament resurrection accounts, but rather Jesus' living identification with the cause of God through his earthly life and ministry. Consequently, we have a hermeneutical circle: "Jesus' living and dying on earth suggested to Christians, in virtue of their experiences after Jesus' death, the idea of the resurrection or of the coming Parousia of Jesus, while on the basis of their faith in the risen or coming crucified One they relate the story of Jesus in the gospels."[32]

Though the earthly ministry of Jesus was a work of self-forgetting, God "remembers" Jesus and such remembrance produces the resurrection and parousia (return). Alternatively, God actually identified the Kingdom with

Jesus of Nazareth. An upshot of this is that the Christian affirmation is not a system but a "living experience of encounter with Jesus of Nazareth"[33] like the encounter the disciples had with Jesus after his death.

Second, in pursuit of his general thesis that Jesus' earthly life was most important to the New Testament authors, Schillebeeckx shows in the primitive Christian creeds the connections made between the one confessed and the earthly Jesus. Among the conclusions he reaches are that (1) there was no creed or *kērygma* ("proclamation") in primitive Christianity not based on some aspect of Jesus' earthly life; (2) all the early Christologies were faith responses to the permanent and definitive significance of Jesus; (3) it is the person of Jesus, not just his message or resurrection, that is the center of the creeds; (4) the heart of Christianity is the persistent eschatological relevance of Jesus' person; and (5) the divers Christologies of the New Testament share a "true to life (faith-motivated) reflection or mirroring of the historical role enacted by Jesus of Nazareth."[34]

On the direct interpretation of the resurrection itself, Schillebeeckx stresses the difference between the New Testament and late Jewish ideas. For the New Testament, Jesus' resurrection is a saving act in itself, God's "amen" to the person of Jesus, and it is precisely *God's* action that raises Jesus from the dead. After discussing at length the "third day" on which that raising occurred, Schillebeeckx concludes that the early Christian affirmation of resurrection on the third day meant that "God's rule has assumed the aspect of the crucified-and-risen-One, Jesus of Nazareth."[35]

Under the customary forms of human history, that is, *not* in an apocalyptic way, the third day continues as a future charged with hope. Neither it nor the other ele-

ments of the doctrine of the resurrection, such as exalta-
tion, sending of the Spirit, and the parousia, depend on
Jesus' empty tomb or his appearances after his death.
Rather, the Jewish context provided models for consider-
ing Jesus actually and truly living with God. It was the
realization that Jesus' deliverance to God had conquered
death which impelled the early Christian communities to
belief in the resurrection. Resurrection thus came to jus-
tify the coming parousia, arrival of God's all-powerful rule.
History may seem to go on as it did before Jesus, but faith
says that in Jesus' crucifixion and resurrection God's definitive action stands accomplished. Thus, Jesus Christ is himself God's powerful rule. "He is the latter-day and definitive revelation of God and in being so is at the same time
the paradigm for an 'eschatological humanity.' "[36]

Though other interpreters of the resurrection do not
subscribe to all of Schillebeeckx' theses, nor place on the
early church's reminiscence of the historical Jesus the
weight he does, the mainstream agrees that the resurrection is not "historical" in the usual sense. That is Küng's
position, as we saw, and it is Rahner's position as well,
insofar as he stresses the unique character of the resurrection event: "If by historically accessible facts is understood
something which in itself and in its own existence belongs
to the realm of our normal, empirical world of time and
space as a phenomenon which occurs *frequently*, then it
is obvious that the resurrection of Jesus neither can be nor
intends to be a 'historical' event."[37]

Speaking for New Testament scholars, Reginald Fuller
has recently reported the following areas of agreement:
First, "there is a remarkable unanimity that the tradition
in 1 Cor 15:3 ff. forms the sole reliable basis for reconstructing the history of the first Easter." Second, "there is
widespread and growing consensus in Germany, Britain

and in this country, that the empty tomb is what Bultmann called a 'late legend.' " On the question of historicity, Fuller believes that "the resurrection is *not* definable as an historical event because its occurrence was not actually witnessed or at least no one claimed to have witnessed it; its occurrence is not actually narrated in the New Testament; and it is attested to only in kerygmatic assertion." These are textual reasons, but he has a theological reason as well, namely, that the resurrection is by definition an eschatological event and so occurs where history stops, at history's "end."[38] This does not mean, as Bultmann suggested, that nothing happened. It means rather that the New Testament wants to say in mythological language that in the resurrection God created a new eschatological existence for Jesus, an existence outside this age. The resurrection is unique.

LIBERATION CHRISTOLOGY

Jon Sobrino's *Christology at the Crossroads* appeared as the Christological equivalent to Gustavo Gutiérrez' *A Theology of Liberation*. Written in troubled El Salvador, it shows dimensions of Jesus which revolutionary faith both needs and appreciates. Like Latin-American liberation theology in general, *Christology at the Crossroads* is motivated by the conviction that practice ought to dominate theory. With political consequences especially in mind, Sobrino states his own Christological position: "The only way to get to know Jesus is to follow after him in one's own real life; to try to identify oneself with his own historical concerns; and to try to fashion his kingdom in our midst. In other words, only through Christian praxis is it possible for us to draw close to Jesus. Following Jesus is the precondition for knowing Jesus."[39] Though Sobrino accepts current critical approaches to Jesus, he adds the liberationist twist that it is Jesus' own praxis which ought to take center stage. Of major European theologians Sobrino is closest to Moltmann, whose concentration on suffering and politics parallels Latin-American concerns.

After these preliminary questions, Sobrino turns to Jesus in his service of the Kingdom, faith, prayer, and death and resurrection. In Sobrino's reading, Matthew 11:5 shows that for Jesus the Kingdom meant "the transformation of a bad situation, of an oppressive situation, and that God's activity can only be envisioned as the *overcoming* of a negative situation." Relatedly, sin is the rejection of God's Kingdom in the self-affirmation that closes people to God and makes them oppress other human beings. Jesus' faith was rooted in his complete dedication to his Father and showed special sensitivity to the structural injustices which dehumanized many of his contemporaries. Thus Sobrino calls the basic moral vision that Jesus gives us "re-creative justice."[40]

The prayer of Jesus was distinctive in that it was directed to his Father. The cross shows how God made the prayer and life of Jesus show us where salvation is in a world of sin and oppression. The suffering of the cross is of the very nature of God: "A truly historical theology of liberation must view suffering as a mode of being belonging to God."[41] Thus, God lives, historically, not in beauty, power, or wisdom, but with and in the oppressed.

Jesus died for seeking the power of a love that was concrete and thus "political." But God suffered with Jesus through to the resurrection, and in the resurrection God answers our questions about what we may hope, what history means, and how we are to live. The consequences of such a faith life draw Sobrino away from cultic worship: "Christian faith also rejects the idea that there is any direct access to God in cultic worship. It can come only indirectly through service to human beings, specifically to those who can represent and embody the total otherness of God in historical terms, namely, the poor and oppressed."[42] It is by returning to the historical Jesus, and avoiding a one-sided focus on the risen Jesus, that we can achieve true faith.

José Miranda's *Being and the Messiah,* although actually a reading of the Johannine literature, begins with a quotation from Jean-Paul Sartre: "To fire workers because a factory is closing is a sovereign act that tacitly assumes the fundamental right to kill." Miranda then appreciatively reviews existentialist, Marxist, and atheistic thought for the political humanism of each, their concern over alienation and oppression. The relation to Christ emerges when views of Kierkegaard and Heidegger on time are replaced by those of the New Testament. The emphasis of Jesus on obligations to one's neighbor, as the Johannine reminiscences especially recall it, suggests to Miranda that:

> Speaking abstractly and formalistically, one is tempted to say that the Epistle's central thesis is that there is only one sign of divine life—whatever that sign may be. What that sign is cannot be resolved by "uniting" belief and love, by "conjoining" dogma and morality; rather it must be resolved by showing that Christological belief is *identical* to the imperative of love of neighbor.[43]

Behind this interpretation is the conviction that "the only legitimate object of Christian theology is the testimony of Jesus Christ." From this testimony comes the new being, the arrived future, that the Johannine writings spotlight. For Miranda the new being has many affinities with the Marxist-existentialist-atheistic hope he has surveyed. The implication of the Johannine new being for faith is

that we *can* live justly, lovingly, if we open ourselves to
what God has done. Those who are "born of God" show
this openness by loving their neighbors and doing justice
to them. Opposed to God is the "world." Thus, the conflict
between God's people and the world turns on their respective works and has its origins in Christ:

> John 7:7 is important because it explicitly tells us *why*
> the world hates Christ: "because I give testimony that
> its works are evil." The world did not believe in Jesus
> because it hates him, and it hates him because he
> testifies that its actions are antithetical to giving food
> to the hungry, drink to the thirsty, clothes to the
> naked, a home to the homeless.[44]

The Johannine Christ signs a warrant for the world's arrest
and destruction.

Through an analysis of the biblical "word," Miranda
shows that Jesus Christ is but the enfleshment of God's
long-standing demand that we do justice. It was the overwhelming mistake of "Christianity" not to center itself in
this message and correlate it with firm faith that Jesus is
the Messiah. Christianity has not really believed that faith
and justice can transform the physical condition of humanity. Where the Johannine Scriptures proclaimed that God
now is so present, historical Christianity preferred a
tamer, less revolutionary God.

Condensing his argument, Miranda focuses on John 17:3
("And this is eternal life, that they know thee the only true
God, and Jesus Christ whom thou hast sent"):

> John 17:3, with its genuinely biblical expression "the
> one true God," in no way is an exception among the
> biblical passages in which this expression appears.
> Eternal life consists in knowing the true God—as dis-
> tinguished from the false gods and mental constructs
> we invent to elude God—and in knowing Jesus as

Christ, that is, as Messiah. John 17:3 is really the summary of the entire message of John and of the New Testament.[45]

The key quality of eternal life is that it does not know death. Believing the "fact" that Jesus is the Messiah, one gains access both to this life and to the power to fulfill God's imperative that we love our neighbor. The stress in all such Johannine discussion is the present, and faith in Jesus as Messiah shows why that should be so. If Jesus has made possible a new being that does not know death, then we need not wait for a future parousia. For Miranda, Johannine Christology proclaims a fully realized eschatology. The parousia is now.

CHAPTER 7

Theology for the 1980s

We have now examined the major areas of recent theological concern. In doing so, we have found, among other things, that discussion of theological method focuses on the relationship of Scripture to critical reason. Scripture continues to be the place where Christians find the paradigmatic experiences of their religious traditions, and all but fundamentalist theologians believe that meeting the demands of critical reason is intrinsic to their profession.

The theology of nature reminded us that whether a universe of staggering immensity is divine, and if so, where we are to locate its divinity, remain hard questions. One of the biggest issues for this aspect of theology in the 1980s seems also to be to clarify the ecological crisis and thus help resolve it. Further, the destruction we visit upon nature is obviously inseparable from the blight of our cities and the sickness of our selves. The self suffers social ills, as it suffers ecological ones. The God of a hopeful decade will be one for all persons, male and female, Christian and non-Christian. The human task in the 1980s is to advance into God's future. The task of theology is to point the way. The Jesus of theology in the 1980s therefore seems likely to be an absolute savior and a liberator. These expressions highlight his decisiveness. For Christians, he is the way, the truth, and the light of both theory and practice. Without diluting God's mystery, Jesus humanizes it. Early Christian belief expressed this in terms of Jesus' Messiahship and divine Sonship. If Jesus is to make Christian faith the access to health and sacredness that it traditionally has been, he has to be decisive and eschatological. This means a "high" Christology of a Jesus who decisively manifests God.

Christian theology in the 1980s therefore must attack the speculative and practical problems of a new high Christology. Karl Rahner has discussed Christ in relation to an evolutionary world.[1] Others must relate Christ to the experiences, symbols, and insights that make us human. In the love which his Father provided, Jesus found the energy to be human. His words flowed from the depths of his love; his deeds burst forth from it. For the author of the Gospel of John, those deeds were signs or sacraments of God's powerful presence. Love, *agapē,* should have priority in Christology, in that it is the very constitution of both "divinity" and "humanity."

With the Jesus of a high Christology as its hermeneutical key, Christian theology could conceive faith as the theory and practice of the twofold commandment of love. In consequence of this, Christian theology could more become a passionate commitment to understand and follow Jesus. Creative theology, like creative science or art, is a work of passionate personal involvement.

Through suffering the love of Christ brought about redemption. The intimacy with God that made Jesus beautiful, and human beings beautiful to Jesus, led to crucifixion. If we are doing Christian theology, we stand in the faith that God's living disclosure is in the way Jesus bore himself, the way he regarded his God and neighbors, and the fate to which the Spirit led him.

Jesus defined himself in terms of a parental God. From political theology, non-Christian religions, and contemplative experience comes a demand to rethink this God's otherness. As the heavens are far from the earth, so God's ways and God's love are far from our own. It is not that God is far away physically. This is not what the crisis of secularity centrally suggests. It is that God is creatively, experientially, and morally distant from the ways we use our time and the ways we use our minds.

Consider, for instance, God's justice. Though Jesus suffered by God's permissive will, he was yet God's beloved. It is axiomatic for the New Testament that the Father raised Jesus from the dead. In any drawing of sides, God clearly stands with those dispossessed like Jesus. Thus, God stands with those who have their treasure in heaven, who give their lives for their neighbors. Christianity cares little for the idols the world thinks important or realistic. Jesus' God of spirit, truth, and love is far from these.

Infrareligious dialogue with Hindu theology today suggests that passivity and activity both impressed Indian divines. Indeed, the androgynous portrayal of Indian divinity was in part an effort to locate "feminine" activity and "masculine" passivity in the ultimate. India also provided yogic experience which sensed the impersonal One without rejecting the emotional love with which the common people prayed. Krishna, the most popular manifestation of Vishnu, made this the highest revelation. By symbolic implication, at least, it had as its source the Hindu trinity of creation, preservation, and destruction.

Christian theism may rightly prefer its own intuitions, procedures, and ontology. At the experiential roots of them, however, an honest Christian religion may well find there is more to androgyny and impersonalism than one might suspect. If everything we say about the God of Jesus is more untrue than true, then God is different from our images of person and father. God does not think or love as human persons do. In the beyond which borders human understanding God effortlessly harmonizes East and West.

Belatedly, theology in the 1980s should develop a truly contemporary mysticism, an absorption with God as God. A primary resource for this is the Eastern Christian tradition, where appreciation for the divine mystery has always run deep. In contrast to the West, the East has loved the spiritual presence of the divine. Its great theologians allowed no distinction between mystical theology and dogmatic theology. The function they saw in authoritatively defined doctrine was to indicate the proper borders of the mystery, not to explain it. One learned more about God existentially by the way of negation than by reasoning. Thus the "desert" kept a guiding hand on Eastern theology, many of the most influential writers of which were monks.

A similar lesson seems ready to hand in Eastern liturgy. What could not be reasoned could be sung. Whatever the proper liturgical forms are for the contemporary West, we are not likely to confess the truly mysterious God well unless we meet him or her in common prayer. For though the liturgy certainly serves the Word, its theological impact derives from its being a contemplative remembering of God in the present.

In our chapter on the self, we examined feminist analyses. As part and parcel of its problems with high Christology and realized eschatology the church throughout the centuries has suffered doctrinal apprehensions about both sex and women. The self that imaged God was not male or female, as the God of Genesis made us. In our own time, women continue to suffer in their work, their religion, and their sex lives because Christian culture suspects them of weakness. For a frightening percentage of our population, they are not on the same level as men. They may sometimes stand above men on pedestals, but each such unnatural elevation brings with it an at least equal degradation.

Theology in the 1980s must support equal rights in secular and religious society alike. Whether it be ordination or professorship, theology has to make it clear that discrimination is a sin against more than half of God's people.

Lastly, current interest in the life cycle will not soon abate. The theologian will be wise to develop his or her analyses of the self's development in contemplation, sexual relations, and work in concert with the best research. In a horizon of universal grace, where natural tendencies can be the concrete carriers of the Spirit's traditional "gifts," theology has to be the clarifier, helper, and partner of the needs and strengths of every human being.

In regard to society, Christian theologians ought in the 1980s to try to lead the church to demonstrations of community and exemplifications of ways of life that show what Christ's love concretely entails. For example, the church has to show much more clearly than it presently does the opposition between Jesus' life-style and that of American capitalism. Internationally, domestically, and ecologically, capitalism is destructive of life.

A theology of society for the 1980s ought to make an assault on the economic basis of our culture. Insofar as that basis is the profit motive, our society is radically unchristian. There is no way the profit motive can square with the biblical call for justice and the New Testament's commandment of love. Neither conceptually nor practically are these compatible. The function of the church is to embody convictions like these, and the function of theologians is to elucidate them.

The profit motive dominating American society shows its virulence in the economic and ecological devastation the Northern nations visit upon the globe. The profit motive, coupled with color prejudice, has made the American black experience an unrelenting nightmare. It would be a significant agenda, then, for the theology of society in the 1980s merely to try to appropriate black Christians' experience.

In an eloquent contribution to a recent symposium on pluralism, Vincent Harding has pointed the black experience toward a theodicy for American culture. First, Harding rejects the notion that "America" is something finished and that there are established Americans, citizens of the first rank. Second, he shows that black Americans have made a special contribution to showing what America *ought* to be. For example, against the enslaving myths of American white religion, black songs and stories have kept spiritual health alive.[2] Black movements, whether for the abolition of slavery or the return to Africa, have also drawn upon a profound sense that God gives all people a claim on justice. Indeed, in the depression of the 1930s Father Divine claimed that God himself was a southern black sharecropper.

American black theology therefore offers leadership for the social reconstructions which lie ahead. If the older civil religion of our country now seems a shambles, perhaps its worst victims will be the best guides to something new. Having learned what the profit motive means when white racists interpret it, blacks know ways to avoid it. Thus, they now insist on participating in the decisions and programs that affect their destinies, for no nonparticipant system has proved trustworthy. As David Hollenbach's study of human rights,[3] which we discussed in Chapter 3, makes very clear, only when the marginalized receive our

primary attention can we expect real progress toward social health.

The marginalized have earned their right to participate.
It is not something which those in power can grant them
as a gift. In the black case, the religious basis of the right
is in the transformation of suffering which black religion
has often achieved: "Nobody knows the trouble I've seen,
Glory, Glory, hallelujah!" If ever theologians had data on
the law of the cross ready to hand, they surely have it in
black experience. How best for white theologians to interpret this data—whether through dialogue or respectful
listening—is a matter of prudence and tactics. As promot-
ing the feminine "half" of the human soul to full equality
might recast the relationship of God to the self, so black
experience may recast social relations.

In doing this, one could expect a return of the "poor of
Yahweh." Society blames them for their poverty, and they
know little of life's abundance. They have no treasure but
the Master of the universe. Perhaps part of the value of the
poor of Yahweh is to make us take a fresh look at God's
"realism." For, despite all the allure of the Johannine
"new being," it is clear that the eschaton will not arrive
tomorrow. Even if human conversion could realize the
new being, conversion on that scale is not likely to occur.
Realistically, there will continue to be many poor whom
we will have with us. The scriptural judgment that they
are precious to God is both a demand that we make them
precious to us and a call to look beyond this-worldly criteria for blessedness.

Christians concerned about the poor and God's Kingdom ought to find in the theology of the next decade a
strong support. Being a Christian means wholehearted
commitment to love God and neighbor utterly. From the
outset, as we must make more clear, the Christian has to

expect to be in conflict with many of society's values.
There are ways of doing business, regarding nature, using
one's body, and conceiving political processes that simply
are incompatible with Jesus' program of love. Profiteering
and neglect can have no part in the Kingdom. To be sure,
there is always the possibility of forgiveness, but in a theology of society as radical as our next years will require, this
possibility ought to be costly. If this results in a church less
popular with the wealthy and the powerful, theologians
will be doing their job.

Similarly, theologians concerned with ecological questions in the next decade had best counsel their audiences
to expect opposition. For in addition to the fact that Western culture remains fixed on profit, growth, and its current
level of pleasure, there is the further and causal religious
fact that few Christians have any effective appreciation of
their bodies or the natural world. There are things that
people who love their bodies and the earth simply do not
do, and today it is all too clear that abuse is rampant. It is
thus incumbent on Christian theologians, committed to a
God who loves all the good things of creation, to call it to
account.

In the 1980s, theology has to contend with ultimate
issues like these, in all their contemporary and traditional
breadth. From the poisoning of mother's milk to the ontology of human defiance, it must conceive of itself as
nothing less than a faith commitment to Jesus. Against the
central problem of our human tendency to inhumanity, it
must delineate God's solution anew. The only power
stronger than false love is the true love that God actually
is. Thus, the only alternative to denaturing is supernatur-
ing: to be human we must be divinized. This is a very old
reading of the Christian story, as old as II Peter 1:4 and the
theology of Athanasius.

More academically, the theology of the 1980s ought to take pains to cover all five of the reality zones, showing how there is a system and connectedness implicit in sustained theological reflection, how all the principal parts are relational.

Adequacy, decisiveness, correlation are watchwords for theology in the 1980s. But can we specify more than general descriptive or procedural suggestions for it? I believe we can, for we can specify what the faith that theology will serve in the 1980s ought to look like. In my view, it ought to be radical contemplation and a radical politics.

By a radical contemplation I mean passionate attention to God as God—to the radical Mystery whose "I am" founds our lives. The biblical God is Spirit, whom we must worship in spirit and truth. The biblical God is love, whom we must worship by love. Radical contemplation tends toward a simplifying love that goes below images and concepts to bring about an exchange of selves. By a radical politics I mean disclosing that social life is different when one's central command and prime treasure are passionate love of God and neighbor. The world has a different hue when "neighbor" includes all of creation. Radical politics is at bottom bringing this difference to the world in order to transform it.

In the context of present American culture radical contemplation and radical politics go quite directly against the mainstream. We are not a people deeply contemplative and ruthlessly just. We fear both the mystery of God and the contemporary struggle against the evil of exploitation, racism, and sexism. To be a Christian in the 1980s, then, may well be in good measure un-American. On the other hand, insofar as God is the source of human meaning and justice is the substance of human sociability, this could be the redemption of our country's soul.

Notes

Chapter 1. Introduction

1. Reginald M. French, trans., *The Way of a Pilgrim* (Seabury Press, 1965).

2. William Hordern, *New Directions in Theology Today, Vol. I: Introduction* (Westminster Press, 1966), p. 12.

3. Robert McAfee Brown and Gustave Weigel, *An American Dialogue* (Doubleday & Co., 1960); Robert McAfee Brown, *Theology in a New Key* (Westminster Press, 1978).

4. David Tracy, *Blessed Rage for Order* (Seabury Press, 1975).

5. Julian N. Hartt, *Theological Method and Imagination* (Seabury Press, 1977), pp. 18, 19.

6. Gordon D. Kaufman, *An Essay on Theological Method,* rev. ed. (Scholars Press, 1979), pp. 16, 32, 46.

7. Alfred North Whitehead, *Process and Reality* (Harper & Row, Harper Torchbooks, 1960), p. 7. In Whitehead's own words: "The true method of discovery is like the flight of an aeroplane. It starts from the ground of particular observation; it makes a flight in the thin air of imaginative generalization; and it lands again for renewed observation rendered acute by rational interpretation."

8. Kaufman, *An Essay on Theological Method,* p. 65.

9. Tracy, *Blessed Rage for Order,* p. 3.

10. Bernard Lonergan, *Method in Theology* (Seabury Press, 1972), pp. 104–105.

11. Ibid., p. xi.

12. Ibid., pp. 125–145.

13. Eric Voegelin, *Israel and Revelation,* Vol. 1 of *Order and History* (Louisiana State University Press, 1956), p. 1.

14. Ibid., p. 58.

15. See ibid., pp. 183–192; also Voegelin's *Anamnesis* (University of Notre Dame Press, 1978), pp. 147–174. Also Paul Tillich, *Dynamics of Faith* (Harper & Brothers, Harper Torchbooks, 1958), pp. 1–4.

16. John B. Cobb, Jr., and David Ray Griffin, *Process Theology: An Introductory Exposition* (Westminster Press, 1976), p. 155.

17. Phillip E. Berryman, "Latin American Liberation Theology," in Sergio Torres and John Eagleson, eds., *Theology in the Americas* (Orbis Books, 1976), p. 61.

18. Penelope Washbourn, *Becoming Woman* (Harper & Row, 1977), p. 74.

19. Karl Rahner, *Foundations of Christian Faith* (Seabury Press, 1978), pp. 50–51.

20. Hans Küng, *On Being a Christian* (Doubleday & Co., 1976), p. 344.

Chapter 2. Nature and the Ecological Crisis

1. Joseph Sittler, *Essays on Nature and Grace* (Fortress Press, 1972).

2. Quoted by Sittler from Richard Wilbur's poem "Objects."

3. John J. Compton, "Science and God's Action in Nature," in Ian G. Barbour, ed., *Earth Might Be Fair* (Prentice-Hall, 1972), pp. 43, 46.

4. Daniel Day Williams, "Changing Concepts of Nature," in Barbour, *Earth Might Be Fair,* pp. 48–61.

5. Ibid., p. 58.

6. Cobb and Griffin, *Process Theology,* pp. 8–10.

7. A brief exposition of the "primordial" and "consequent" natures of Whitehead's divinity, and of its relation to the natural world, is available in my article, "A Note on the God-World Relation in Whitehead's *Process and Reality,*" *Philosophy Today,* Vol. 15, No. 4 (Winter 1971), pp. 302–312.

8. Cobb and Griffin, *Process Theology,* p. 75.

9. Ibid., p. 118.

10. Lewis S. Ford, *The Lure of God* (Fortress Press, 1978), p. 113. An alternative is to show that for an unlimited divinity good can triumph "no matter what" without our sufferings losing their meaning. This involves insights hammered out in the predestinarian controversies, and a solid grasp on how divine efficacy does not impose necessity on its consequents. See Bernard Lonergan, *Insight* (Philosophical Library, 1957), pp. 657–667.

11. Ford, *The Lure of God,* p. 119.

12. Robin Attfield, "Science and Creation," *The Journal of Religion,* Vol. 58, No. 1 (Jan. 1978), pp. 37–47. Frederick Ferré, "Explanation in Science and Theology," in Barbour, *Earth Might Be Fair,* p. 31.

13. Ferré, "Explanation," in Barbour, *Earth Might Be Fair,* p. 32.

14. Ian G. Barbour, *Myths, Models and Paradigms: A Comparative Study in Science and Religion* (Harper & Row, 1974), pp. 47–48.

15. Ibid., p. 161.

16. Harold K. Schilling, *The New Consciousness in Science and Religion* (United Church Press, 1973).

17. Wolfhart Pannenberg, *Theology and the Philosophy of Science* (Westminster Press, 1976), pp. 134–135, 126, 127.

18. Ibid., p. 134.

19. Ibid., pp. 297, 301.

20. Ibid., p. 310.

21. Stanley L. Jaki, *The Road of Science and the Ways to God* (University of Chicago Press, 1978).

22. Tracy, *Blessed Rage for Order,* pp. 94, 96.

23. Ibid., p. 99.

24. Michael Polanyi, *Personal Knowledge* (Harper & Row, Harper Torchbooks, 1964), especially pp. 69–131, and Jeremy Bernstein, *Einstein* (Viking Press, 1973).

25. Herman E. Daly, ed., *Toward a Steady-State Economy* (W. H. Freeman, 1973); Ian G. Barbour et al., eds., *Finite Resources and the Human Future* (Augsburg Publishing House, 1976); American Academy of Arts and Sciences, *When Values Conflict* (Ballinger Pub. Co., 1976).

26. Nicholas Georgescu-Roegen, "The Entropy Law and the Economic Problem," in Daly, *Toward a Steady-State Economy,* pp. 46–47.

27. Preston Cloud, "Mineral Resources in Fact and Fancy," in Daly, *Toward a Steady-State Economy,* p. 74.

28. Paul R. Ehrlich and John P. Hodern, "Impact of Population Growth," in Daly, *Toward a Steady-State Economy,* pp. 76–77, 87.

29. Jorgen Randers and Donella Meadows, "The Carrying Capacity of Our Global Environment," in Daly, *Toward a Steady-State Economy,* pp. 283–306, 283.

30. Donella Meadows, "Panel on Food Population," in Barbour, *Finite Resources,* pp. 55–56.

31. See Herman E. Daly, "Electric Power, Unemployment,

and Economic Growth," in Daly, *Toward a Steady-State Economy*, pp. 252–277.

32. Barbara Ward, *Progress for a Small Planet* (W. W. Norton & Co., 1979), p. 69.

33. David Spring and Eileen Spring, eds., *Ecology and Religion in History* (Harper & Row, Harper Torchbooks, 1974).

34. James Barr, "Man and Nature: The Ecological Controversy and the Old Testament," in Spring and Spring, *Ecology and Religion*, pp. 48–75.

35. Lewis W. Moncrief, "The Cultural Basis for Our Environmental Crisis," in Spring, *Ecology and Religion*, pp. 76–90.

36. Yi-Fu Tuan, "Discrepancies Between Environmental Attitude and Behaviour," in Spring and Spring, *Ecology and Religion*, pp. 101–104.

37. René Dubos, "Franciscan Conservationism Versus Benedictine Stewardship," in Spring and Spring, *Ecology and Religion*, pp. 114–136.

38. Garrett Hardin, "Lifeboat Ethics: Food and Population," in Barbour, *Finite Resources*, p. 41.

39. Roger Shinn, "Lifeboat Ethics: A Response," in Barbour, *Finite Resources*, p. 51.

40. Paul Santmire, "Ecology, Justice, and Theology," *The Christian Century*, Vol. 92, No. 17 (May 12, 1976), pp. 460–464.

41. See Marie Augusta Neal, *A Socio-Theology of Letting Go* (Paulist Press, 1977).

42. See Roland Marstin, "A Look at 'Theology in the Americas,' " *Christianity and Crisis*, Vol. 38, No. 12 (Aug. 21, 1978), pp. 198–200.

43. William R. LaFleur, "Saigyo and the Buddhist Value of Nature," *History of Religions*, Vol. 13, No. 2 (Nov. 1973), pp. 93–128; Vol. 13, No. 3 (Feb. 1974), pp. 227–248.

44. See E. F. Schumacher, *Small Is Beautiful* (Harper & Row, Harper Colophon Books, 1973). Also his *A Guide for the Perplexed* (Harper & Row, Harper Colophon Books, 1977), and *Good Work* (Harper & Row, 1979), pp. 256–273.

45. Schumacher, *Small Is Beautiful*, pp. 51, 54.

Chapter 3. Society and Church

1. Arnold Toynbee, *Mankind and Mother Earth* (Oxford University Press, 1976).

2. *Times Atlas of World History*, ed. Geoffrey Barraclough (Hammond, 1979).

3. Toynbee, *Mankind and Mother Earth*, pp. 589–596.

4. Eric Voegelin, *The Ecumenic Age,* Vol. 4 of *Order and History* (Louisiana State University Press, 1975).

5. Langdon Gilkey, *Reaping the Whirlwind* (Seabury Press, 1976).

6. Ibid., p. 264.

7. William A. Clebsch, *Christianity in European History* (Oxford University Press, 1979), p. 6.

8. Ibid., pp. 242, 281.

9. Robert Coles, *Privileged Ones* (Little, Brown & Co., 1977), pp. 548–549.

10. Ibid.

11. Ibid., p. 553.

12. Avery Dulles, "Jus Divinum as Ecumenical Problem," *Theological Studies,* Vol. 38, No. 4 (Dec. 1977), pp. 681–708.

13. Ibid., p. 699.

14. Ibid., p. 705.

15. Michael A. Fahey, "Orthodox Ecumenism and Theology: 1970–78," *Theological Studies,* Vol. 39, No. 3 (Sept. 1978), pp. 446–485.

16. Alexander Schmemann, "The East and West May Yet Meet," in Peter Berger and Richard John Neuhaus, eds., *Against the World for the World: The Hartford Appeal and the Future of American Religion* (Seabury Press, 1976), p. 128.

17. Robert A. Evans, "Theological Brief," in Robert A. Evans and Thomas D. Parker, eds., *Christian Theology: A Case Method Approach* (Harper & Row, Harper Torchbooks, 1976), p. 199.

18. Richard P. McBrien, "Theological Brief," in Evans and Parker, *Christian Theology,* p. 204.

19. Bernard Cooke, *Ministry to Word and Sacraments* (Fortress Press, 1976).

20. Ibid., p. 214.

21. Ibid., pp. 320, 339.

22. James F. White, *Christian Worship in Transition* (Abingdon Press, 1976), pp. 131–142.

23. Juan Luis Segundo, *The Liberation of Theology* (Orbis Books, 1976); José Miranda, *Marx and the Bible* (Orbis Books, 1974), also *Being and the Messiah* (Orbis Books, 1977); Dorothee Soelle, *Political Theology* (Fortress Press, 1974), especially pp. 83–92.

24. Torres and Eagleson, *Theology in the Americas.*

25. Brown, *Theology in a New Key.*

26. See Frederick Lawrence, "Political Theology and the Longer Cycle of Decline," in Frederick Lawrence, ed., *Lonergan Workshop: Vol. I* (Scholars Press, 1978), pp. 223–255.

27. James M. Gustafson, *Protestant and Roman Catholic Ethics* (University of Chicago Press, 1978), p. 148.

28. Ibid., p. 153.

29. David Hollenbach, *Claims in Conflict* (Paulist Press, 1979).

30. Ibid., p. 132.

31. See ibid., p. 200.

32. Ibid., p. 204.

Chapter 4. Self

1. Erik Erikson, "Dr. Borg's Life-Cycle," *Daedalus*, Vol. 105, No. 2 (Spring 1976), pp. 1–28. For Erikson's basic chart of the life-cycle stages, conflicts, and virtues, see p. 22. The Luther and Gandhi studies are: *Young Man Luther* (W. W. Norton & Co., 1958); *Gandhi's Truth* (W. W. Norton & Co., 1969). As evidence of Erikson's influence on other scholars of religion, see the other essays in the *Daedalus* issue, and also Donald Capps et al., eds., *Encounter with Erikson* (Scholars Press, 1977). Pages 421–429 of this latter work are a bibliography of Erikson's books and articles from 1930 to 1975. The script of *Wild Strawberries* is available in Ingmar Bergman, *Four Screenplays* (1960).

2. Erikson, "Dr. Borg's Life-Cycle," pp. 25, 24.

3. Ibid., p. 23.

4. Donald Capps, *Pastoral Care* (Westminster Press, 1979).

5. Paul W. Pruyser, *The Minister as Diagnostician* (Westminster Press, 1976).

6. Capps, *Pastoral Care*, p. 115.

7. Ibid., pp. 127, 129.

8. Evelyn Whitehead and James Whitehead, *Christian Life Patterns* (Doubleday & Co., 1979).

9. Daniel Levinson, *The Seasons of a Man's Life* (Alfred A. Knopf, 1978).

10. Elie Wiesel, *The Gates of the Forest* (Avon Books, 1966).

11. John Shea, *Stories of God* (Thomas More Press, 1978), p. 11.

12. Ibid., pp. 12–13.

13. Ibid., pp. 38–39.

14. Dorothy Dinnerstein, *The Mermaid and the Minotaur* (Harper & Row, Harper Colophon Books, 1977), pp. 4, 5.

15. Ibid., p. 26.

16. Ibid., p. 208.

17. Ibid., p. 213.

18. *Commonweal Papers No. 6,* Vol. 105, No. 12 (June 16, 1978), pp. 380–386, 386–392.

19. Richard McCormick, "Notes on Moral Theology: 1978," *Theological Studies,* Vol. 40, No. 1 (March 1979), pp. 59–112.

20. Peter Hebblethwaite, *The National Catholic Reporter,* Vol. 16, No. 3 (Nov. 9, 1979), p. 2.

21. Rosemary Radford Ruether, "Home and Work," *Theological Studies,* Vol. 36, No. 4 (Dec. 1975), pp. 647–659.

22. Ibid., pp. 658, 659.

23. John McMurtry, *The Structure of Marx's World-View* (Princeton University Press, 1978), pp. 19–53.

24. Karl Marx, *Grundrisse,* trans. and ed. Martin Nicolaus (Penguin Books, 1973), p. 706. Quoted by McMurtry on p. 29.

25. Karl Marx, *Critique of the Gotha Program* (Progress Publishers, 1966), p. 17. Quoted by McMurtry on p. 32.

26. Louise Kapp Howe, *Pink Collar Workers* (Avon Books, 1977).

27. Studs Terkel, *Working* (Pantheon Books, 1974), p. xi.

28. Ibid., p. xxiv.

29. Schumacher, *Good Work,* p. 125.

30. Ibid., p. 126.

31. Ibid., p. 138.

32. Ibid., p. 142.

33. Sergius Bolshakoff and M. Basil Pennington, *In Search of True Wisdom* (Doubleday & Co., 1979).

34. Ibid., p. 110.

35. See M. Basil Pennington, *Daily We Touch Him* (Doubleday & Co., 1977).

36. See William Johnston, ed., *The Cloud of Unknowing* (Doubleday & Co., 1973); William Johnston, *The Still Point: Reflections on Zen and Christian Mysticism* (Harper & Row, 1971); William Johnston, *The Inner Eye of Love* (Harper & Row, 1978), p. 135.

37. Morton Kelsey, *The Other Side of Silence* (Paulist Press, 1976), p. 130.

Chapter 5. God

1. Herbert Vorgrimler, "Recent Critiques of Theism," in Edward Schillebeeckx and B. van Iersel, eds., *A Personal God* (Seabury Press, 1977), pp. 23–34.

2. Ibid., p. 27. The works of Soelle to which Vorgrimler refers are *Truth Is Concrete* (Herder & Herder, 1969) and *Das Recht* (Neuwied, 1971).

3. Ibid., p. 32.

4. Samuel Terrien, *The Elusive Presence* (Harper & Row, 1978), p. 476.

5. Charles Birch, "Nature, God and Humanity in Ecological Perspective," *Christianity and Crisis*, Vol. 39, No. 16 (Oct. 29, 1979), p. 262.

6. John A. Coleman, "Situation for Modern Faith," *Theological Studies*, Vol. 39, No. 4 (Dec. 1978), p. 631.

7. Guy Swanson, "Modern Secularity," in Donald Cutler, ed., *The Religious Situation 1969* (Beacon Press, 1969), pp. 829–830. Coleman quotes this on p. 632.

8. Berger and Neuhaus, *Against the World for the World.*

9. Alexander Schmemann, "The East and West May Yet Meet," in Berger and Neuhaus, *Against the World for the World*, pp. 126–137.

10. Avery Dulles, "Unmasking Secret Infidelities: Hartford and the Future of Ecumenism," in Berger and Neuhaus, *Against the World for the World*, p. 59.

11. Richard J. Mouw, "New Alignments: Hartford and the Future of Evangelicalism," in Berger and Neuhaus, *Against the World for the World*, p. 99.

12. Ibid., p. 108.

13. The reference is to Pannenberg's article, "Breaking Ground for Renewed Faith," *Worldview*, Vol. 18, No. 6 (June 1975), pp. 37–38.

14. Peter Berger, "Secular Theology and the Rejection of the Supernatural: Reflections on Recent Trends," *Theological Studies*, Vol. 38, No. 1 (March 1977), p. 49.

15. Langdon Gilkey, *Catholicism Confronts Modernity: A Protestant View* (Seabury Press, 1975), p. 59. Berger quotes this on p. 47.

16. Berger, "Secular Theology and the Rejection of the Supernatural," p. 56.

17. Langdon Gilkey, Schubert M. Ogden, David Tracy, "Responses to Peter Berger," *Theological Studies*, Vol. 39, No. 3 (Sept. 1978), p. 496.

18. Langdon Gilkey, *Message and Existence* (Seabury Press, 1979).

19. Ibid., p. 91.

20. Ibid., p. 92.

21. Ibid., pp. 94, 95.

22. Ibid., p. 96.

23. Louis Dupré, *The Other Dimension* (Seabury Press, 1979). See especially pp. 275–328.

24. John Macquarrie, *Principles of Christian Theology,* rev. ed. (London: SCM Press, 1977), especially p. 115.

25. Ibid., pp. 121, 122.

26. Ninian Smart, "Understanding Religious Experience," in Steven Katz, ed., *Mysticism and Philosophical Analysis* (Oxford University Press, 1978), p. 20.

27. John Bowker, *The Sense of God* (Oxford: Clarendon Press, 1973).

28. John Bowker, *The Religious Imagination and the Sense of God* (Oxford: Clarendon Press, 1978), p. 315.

29. Ibid.

30. Raimundo Panikkar, *The Intrareligious Dialogue* (Paulist Press, 1978). *Cross Currents,* Vol. 29, No. 2 (Summer 1979), is devoted to Panikkar's work.

31. Ibid., p. 2.

32. Ibid., p. 3.

33. Ibid., pp. 4–5.

34. Ibid., p. 14.

35. Ibid., p. 91.

36. Rita Gross, ed., *Beyond Androcentrism* (Scholars Press, 1977); Gael Hodgkins, "Sedna: Images of the Transcendent in an Eskimo Goddess," pp. 305–314; Joanna Rodgers Macy, "Perfection of Wisdom: Mother of All Buddhas," pp. 325–333.

37. C. N. Tay, "Kuan-yin: The Cult of Half Asia," *History of Religions,* Vol. 16, No. 2 (Nov. 1976), pp. 147–177; Ellen Marie Chen, "Tao as the Great Mother and the Influence of Motherly Love in the Shaping of Chinese Philosophy," *History of Religions,* Vol. 14, No. 1 (Aug. 1974), pp. 51–63; Rita Gross, "Hindu Female Deities as a Resource for the Contemporary Rediscovery of the Goddess," *Journal of the American Academy of Religion,* Vol. 46, No. 3 (Sept. 1978), pp. 269–291; David Kinsley, "The Portrait of the Goddess in the Devimahatmya," *Journal of the American Academy of Religion,* Vol. 46, No. 4 (Dec. 1978), pp. 489–506; Stella Kramrisch, "The Indian Great Goddess," *History of Religions,* Vol. 14, No. 4 (May 1975), pp. 235–265.

38. Judith Plaskow, "The Feminist Transformation of Theology," in Gross, *Beyond Androcentrism,* p. 24. Valerie Goldstein, "The Human Situation: A Feminist View," *The Journal of Religion,* Vol. 40, No. 2 (April 1960), pp. 100–112.

39. Plaskow, "Feminist Transformation," in Gross, *Beyond Androcentrism,* p. 26.

40. Phyllis Trible, *God and the Rhetoric of Sexuality* (Fortress Press, 1978).

41. Ibid., pp. 102, 162.

42. Ibid., p. 196.

Chapter 6. Christology

1. David Kelsey, *The Uses of Scripture in Recent Theology* (Fortress Press, 1975), p. 205.

2. Edward Schillebeeckx, *Jesus: An Experiment in Christology* (Seabury Press, 1979), p. 22.

3. Hartt, *Theological Method and Imagination*, p. 132.

4. Norman Perrin, *Jesus and the Language of the Kingdom* (Fortress Press, 1976), p. 5.

5. John B. Cobb, Jr., with David J. Lull and Barry A. Woodbridge, "Introduction: Process Thought and New Testament Exegesis," *Journal of the American Academy of Religion*, Vol. 47, No. 1 (March 1979), pp. 24, 25.

6. Ibid., p. 24.

7. Bernard Lonergan, "Christology Today: Methodological Reflections," in Michel Gervais and Raymond LaFlamme, eds., *Le Christ Hier, Aujourd'hui, et Demain* (Quebec: Les Presses de l'Université Laval, 1977), p. 56.

8. Ibid., p. 57.

9. Ibid., p. 58.

10. Stephen Neill, *Jesus Through Many Eyes* (Fortress Press, 1976), p. 164.

11. Géza Vermès, *Jesus the Jew* (London: Fontana/Collins, 1976), p. 223.

12. Ibid., p. 224.

13. Ibid., p. 225.

14. Milan Machoveč, *A Marxist Looks at Jesus* (Fortress Press, 1976).

15. Ibid., p. 87.

16. Ibid., p. 89.

17. Lucas Grollenberg, *Jesus* (Westminster Press, 1978), p. 103.

18. J. L. Houlden, *Ethics and the New Testament* (Oxford University Press, 1977).

19. Perrin, *Jesus and the Language of the Kingdom*, p. 142; Daniel O. Via, *The Parables: Their Literary and Existential Dimension* (Fortress Press, 1967).

20. Perrin, *Jesus and the Language of the Kingdom*, pp. 157–158.

21. Beardslee, "Parable, Proverb, and Koan," in William A.

Beardslee, ed., *The Poetics of Faith* (Scholars Press, 1978), pp. 151–177; "Saving One's Life by Losing It," *Journal of the American Academy of Religion*, Vol. 47, No. 1 (March 1979), pp. 57–72.

22. Beardslee, "Parable, Proverb, and Koan," in Beardslee, *The Poetics of Faith*, pp. 152, 156.

23. Beardslee, "Saving One's Life by Losing It," p. 69.

24. Ford, *The Lure of God*, p. 49.

25. Ibid., p. 79.

26. Ibid., p. 86.

27. See Walter Kasper, *Jesus the Christ* (Paulist Press, 1977), p. 22.

28. Ibid., p. 249.

29. Küng, *On Being a Christian*, p. 125.

30. Ibid., p. 214.

31. Ibid., pp. 335, 351.

32. Edward Schillebeeckx, *Jesus* (Paulist Press, 1979), p. 399.

33. Ibid., p. 402.

34. Ibid., p. 513.

35. Ibid., p. 531.

36. Ibid., p. 544.

37. Rahner, *Foundations of Christian Faith*, p. 277.

38. Reginald Fuller, "The Resurrection Narratives in Recent Study," in Thomas J. Ryan, ed., *Critical History and Biblical Faith* (Villanova: The College Theology Society/Horizons, 1979), pp. 93, 101, 103.

39. Jon Sobrino, *Christology at the Crossroads* (Orbis Books, 1978), p. xiii; Gustavo Gutiérrez, *A Theology of Liberation* (Orbis Books, 1973).

40. Sobrino, *Christology at the Crossroads*, pp. 47, 122.

41. Ibid., p. 195.

42. Ibid., p. 227.

43. Miranda, *Being and the Messiah*, pp. 1, 99.

44. Ibid., pp. 80, 99.

45. Ibid., p. 195.

Chapter 7. Theology for the 1980s

1. Rahner, *Foundations of Christian Faith*, pp. 178–203.

2. Vincent Harding, "Out of the Cauldron of Struggle: Black Religion and the Search for a New America," *Soundings*, Vol. 59, No. 3 (Fall 1978), p. 342.

3. Hollenbach, *Claims in Conflict.*

Bibliography

Ahlstrom, Sydney E. *A Religious History of the American People.* Yale University Press, 1972.

Barbour, Ian G. *Myths, Models and Paradigms: A Comparative Study in Science and Religion.* Harper & Row, 1974.

Barbour, Ian G., ed. *Earth Might Be Fair.* Prentice-Hall, 1972.

Barbour, Ian G., et al., eds. *Finite Resources and the Human Future.* Augsburg Publishing House, 1976.

Beardslee, William, ed. *The Poetics of Faith: Essays Offered to Amos Niven Wilder. Semeia* 12 and 13. Scholars Press, 1978.

Berger, Peter, and Neuhaus, Richard John, eds. *Against the World for the World: The Hartford Appeal and the Future of American Religion.* Seabury Press, 1976.

Bolshakoff, Sergius, and Pennington, M. Basil. *In Search of True Wisdom: Visits to Eastern Spiritual Fathers.* Doubleday & Co., 1979.

Bowker, John. *The Religious Imagination and the Sense of God.* Oxford: Clarendon Press, 1978.

————. *The Sense of God.* Oxford: Clarendon Press, 1973.

Brown, Robert McAfee. *Theology in a New Key.* Westminster Press, 1978.

Capps, Donald. *Pastoral Care.* Westminster Press, 1979.

Capps, Donald, et al., eds. *Encounter with Erikson.* Scholars Press, 1977.

Carmody, Denise Lardner. *Women and World Religions.* Abingdon Press, 1979.

Chadwick, Owen. *The Secularization of the European Mind in the Nineteenth Century.* Cambridge University Press, 1975.

Christ, Carol, and Plaskow, Judith, eds. *Womanspirit Rising: A Feminist Reader in Religion.* Harper & Row, 1979.

Clark, Elizabeth, and Richardson, Herbert, eds. *Women and Religion.* Harper & Row, 1977.

Clebsch, William A. *Christianity in European History.* Oxford University Press, 1979.

Cobb, John B., Jr., and Griffin, David Ray. *Process Theology: An Introductory Exposition.* Westminster Press, 1976.

Coles, Robert. *Privileged Ones: The Well-off and the Rich in America* (The Children of Crisis, Vol. 5). Little, Brown & Co., 1977.

Cooke, Bernard. *Ministry to Word and Sacraments.* Fortress Press, 1976.

Daly, Herman E., ed. *Toward a Steady-State Economy.* W. H. Freeman, 1973.

Dinnerstein, Dorothy. *The Mermaid and the Minotaur: Sexual Arrangements and Human Malaise.* Harper & Row, Harper Colophon Books, 1977.

Dudko, Dmitrii. *Our Hope.* St. Vladimir's Seminary Press, 1977.

Dupré, Louis. *The Other Dimension: A Search for the Meaning of Religious Attitudes.* Seabury Press, 1979.

Eliade, Mircea. *From the Stone Age to the Eleusinian Mysteries,* Vol. 1 of *A History of Religious Ideas.* University of Chicago Press, 1978.

Evans, Robert A., and Parker, Thomas D., eds. *Christian Theology: A Case Method Approach.* Harper & Row, Harper Torchbooks, 1976.

Ford, Lewis S. *The Lure of God: A Biblical Background for Process Theism.* Fortress Press, 1978.

Gilkey, Langdon. *Message and Existence: An Introduction to Christian Theology.* Seabury Press, 1979.

———. *Reaping the Whirlwind: A Christian Interpretation of History.* Seabury Press, 1976.

Grollenberg, Lucas. *Jesus.* Westminster Press, 1978.

Gross, Rita, ed. *Beyond Androcentrism: New Essays on Women and Religion.* Scholars Press, 1977.

Gustafson, James M. *Protestant and Roman Catholic Ethics.* University of Chicago Press, 1978.

Hartt, Julian N. *Theological Method and Imagination.* Seabury Press, 1977.

Hollenbach, David. *Claims in Conflict: Retrieving and Renewing the Catholic Human Rights Tradition.* Paulist Press, 1979.

Houlden, J. L. *Ethics and the New Testament.* Oxford University Press, 1977.

Jaki, Stanley L. *The Road of Science and the Ways to God.* University of Chicago Press, 1978.

Johnston, William. *The Inner Eye of Love: Mysticism and Religion.* Harper & Row, 1978.

Kasper, Walter. *Jesus the Christ.* Paulist Press, 1977.

Kaufman, Gordon D. *An Essay on Theological Method.* Rev. ed. Scholars Press, 1979.

Kelsey, David. *The Uses of Scripture in Recent Theology.* Fortress Press, 1975.

Kelsey, Morton. *The Other Side of Silence: A Guide to Christian Meditation.* Paulist Press, 1976.

Küng, Hans. *On Being a Christian.* Doubleday & Co., 1976.

Lawrence, Frederick, ed. *Lonergan Workshop, Vol. I.* Scholars Press, 1978.

Lonergan, Bernard. *Method in Theology.* Seabury Press, 1972.

Lossky, Vladimir. *The Mystical Theology of the Eastern Church.* St. Vladimir's Seminary Press, 1976.

Machoveč, Milan. *A Marxist Looks at Jesus.* Fortress Press, 1976.

McMurtry, John. *The Structure of Marx's World-View.* Princeton University Press, 1978.

Macquarrie, John. *Principles of Christian Theology.* Rev. ed. London: SCM Press, 1977.

Miranda, José. *Being and the Messiah: The Message of St. John.* Orbis Books, 1977.

Neill, Stephen. *Jesus Through Many Eyes: Introduction to the Theology of the New Testament.* Fortress Press, 1976.

Panikkar, Raimundo. *The Intrareligious Dialogue.* Paulist Press, 1978.

Pannenberg, Wolfhart. *Theology and the Philosophy of Science.* Westminster Press, 1976.

Perrin, Norman. *Jesus and the Language of the Kingdom.* Fortress Press, 1976.

Polanyi, Michael, and Prosch, Harry. *Meaning.* University of Chicago Press, 1975.

Rahner, Karl. *Foundations of Christian Faith.* Seabury Press, 1978.

Ricoeur, Paul. *Biblical Hermeneutics. Semeia* 4. Scholars Press, 1975.

Ruether, Rosemary Radford. *New Woman—New Earth.* Seabury Press, 1975.

Schillebeeckx, Edward, and Van Iersel B., eds. *A Personal God.* Seabury Press, 1977.

Schumacher, E. F. *Good Work.* Harper & Row, 1979.

Segundo, Juan Luis. *The Liberation of Theology.* Orbis Books, 1976.

Shea, John. *Stories of God: An Unauthorized Biography.* Thomas More Press, 1978.

Sittler, Joseph. *Essays on Nature and Grace.* Fortress Press, 1972.

Sobrino, Jon. *Christology at the Crossroads.* Orbis Books, 1978.

Soelle, Dorothee. *Political Theology.* Fortress Press, 1974.

Spring, David, and Spring, Eileen, eds. *Ecology and Religion in History.* Harper & Row, Harper Torchbooks, 1974.

Terrien, Samuel. *The Elusive Presence.* Harper & Row, 1978.

TeSelle, Sallie. *Speaking in Parables: A Study in Metaphor and Theology.* Fortress Press, 1975.

Torres, Sergio, and Eagleson, John, eds. *Theology in the Americas.* Orbis Books, 1976.

Toulmin, Stephen. *The Collective Use and Evolution of Concepts,* Vol. 1 of *Human Understanding.* Princeton University Press, 1977.

Toynbee, Arnold. *Mankind and Mother Earth.* Oxford University Press, 1976.

Tracy, David. *Blessed Rage for Order: The New Pluralism in Theology.* Seabury Press, 1975.

Tracy, David, et al., eds. *Towards Vatican III.* Seabury Press, 1978.

Trible, Phyllis. *God and the Rhetoric of Sexuality.* Fortress Press, 1978.

Vermès, Géza. *Jesus the Jew.* London: Fontana/Collins, 1976.

Voegelin, Eric. *The Ecumenic Age,* Vol. 4 of *Order and History.* Louisiana State University Press, 1975.

Ward, Barbara. *Progress for a Small Planet.* W. W. Norton & Co., 1979.

Whitehead, Evelyn, and Whitehead, James. *Christian Life Patterns.* Doubleday & Co., 1979.

Wilmore, Gayraud S., and Cone, James H. *Black Theology: A Documentary History, 1966–1979.* Orbis Books, 1979.

Index of Names